Selected Plays of Padraic Colum

IRISH STUDIES

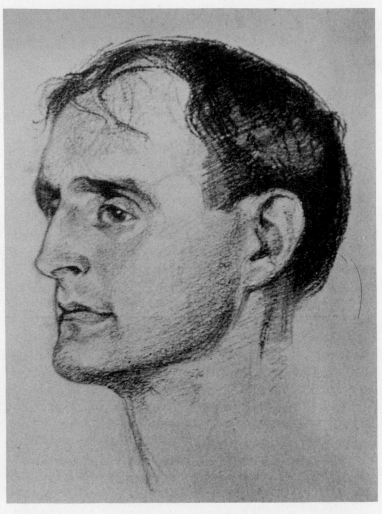

Padraic Colum, ca. 1920, from a drawing by Willy Pogany. *Courtesy of Special Collections, Glenn G. Bartle Library, State University of New York at Binghamton.*

Selected Plays of
PADRAIC COLUM

Edited by

SANFORD STERNLICHT

SYRACUSE UNIVERSITY PRESS   1986

SANFORD STERNLICHT is a poet, critic, historian, and theater director. His books include *Gull's Way* (poetry, 1961); *Love in Pompeii* (poetry, 1967); *John Webster's Imagery and the Webster Canon* (1972); *John Masefield* (1977); *C. S. Forester* (1981); *Padraic Colum* (1985); and the *Selected Short Stories of Padraic Colum* (Syracuse University Press, 1985). He is also the author of four books on American naval history of which *McKinley's Bulldog: The Battleship Oregon* (1977) was a Military Book Club and *Saturday Evening Post* Book Club selection. Professor Sternlicht is an adjunct member of the English Department of Syracuse University.

Library of Congress Cataloging-in-Publication Data

Colum, Padraic, 1881–1972.
  Selected plays of Padraic Colum.

  (Irish studies)
  Contents: The land—The betrayal—Glendalough—
[etc.]
    I. Sternlicht, Sanford V. II. Title. III. Series:
Irish studies (Syracuse University. Press)
PR6005.O38A6   1986b   822'.912   86-22973
ISBN 0-8156-2386-0 (alk. paper)

CONTENTS

INTRODUCTION   vii

THE LAND   3

THE BETRAYAL   39

GLENDALOUGH   59

MONASTERBOICE   87

IRISH STUDIES

Irish Studies presents a wide range of books interpreting important aspects of Irish life and culture to scholarly and general audiences. The richness and complexity of the Irish experience, past and present, deserves broad understanding and careful analysis. For this reason an important purpose of the series is to offer a forum to scholars interested in Ireland, its history, and culture. Irish literature is a special concern in the series, but works from the perspectives of the fine arts, history, and the social sciences are also welcome, as are studies which take multidisciplinary approaches.

Irish Studies is a continuing project of Syracuse University Press and is under the general editorship of Richard Fallis, associate professor of English at Syracuse University.

Irish Studies, edited by Richard Fallis

Children's Lore in Finnegans Wake. Grace Eckley

The Drama of J. M. Synge. Mary C. King

Fionn mac Cumhaill: Celtic Myth in English Literature. James MacKillop

Great Hatred, Little Room: The Irish Historical Novel. James M. Cahalan

Hanna Sheehy-Skeffington: Irish Feminist. Leah Levenson and Jerry Natterstad

In Minor Keys: The Uncollected Short Stories of George Moore. Edited by David B. Eakin and Helmut E. Gerber

Ireland Sober, Ireland Free: Drink and Temperance in Nineteenth-Century Ireland. Elizabeth Malcolm

Irish Life and Traditions. Edited by Sharon Gmelch

The Irish Renaissance. Richard Fallis

The Literary Vision of Liam O'Flaherty. John N. Zneimer

Northern Ireland: The Background to the Conflict, Edited by John Darby

Peig: The Autobiography of Peig Sayers of the Great Blasket Island. Translated by Bryan MacMahon

Selected Plays of Padraic Colum. Edited by Sanford Sternlicht

Selected Short Stories of Padraic Colum. Edited by Sanford Sternlicht

Shadowy Heroes: Irish Literature of the 1890s. Wayne E. Hall

Ulster's Uncertain Defenders: Protestant Political, Paramilitary and Community Groups and the Northern Ireland Conflict. Sarah Nelson

Yeats. Douglas Archibald

INTRODUCTION

ALL HIS LONG, PRODUCTIVE LIFE Padraic Colum (1881–1972) thought of himself as a dramatist, although the literary world regarded him primarily as a lyric poet and he earned most of his living as a writer of children's books and a compiler of anthologies. But early recognition came to Colum from the stage, with the Irish National Theatre Society, whose first president was William Butler Yeats, and in one of modern theater's great repertory institutions, the Abbey Theatre. As late as 1969 Colum said to his friend Charles Burgess, "I am primarily a man of the theatre and always have been. . . . If I am not a playwright, I am nothing."[1] Whatever he wrote, be it poem, play, story, novel, biography, or children's book, a dramatist's imagination energized his work with directness, clarity, a logical structure, and perduring vision behind simple words.

Colum liked to tell people that he was Roman Catholic, of peasant stock, and had been born in the workhouse in Longford. It was all true with the modification that his father, Patrick Collumb, graduate of the National School, was, like Colum's character Thomas Muskerry, the workhouse master. Padraic, christened Patrick after his father, was the first of eight children born to the workhouse master and his wife, Susan, a gardener's daughter who would die worn out after the birth of her last child and whom Colum would remember always as a beautiful, generous, loving woman. Her husband, a gentleman of considerable thirst, lost his position, left his family with their maternal grandmother in County Cavan, emigrated to America, failed there also, and returned to Ireland, finding employment as a clerk in the Sandycove railway station just outside of Dublin. When he rose to the rank of station master, he obtained employment for his eldest son with the railway. Colum had had only eight years of formal education.

Colum soon passed an examination for clerk with the Irish Railway Clearing House on Kildare Street, Dublin, where he worked a nine-hour-a-day, six-day-a-week shift for five years, writing plays and poems in his spare time and assuming some of the financial burden of caring for his younger brothers and sisters when his father, still imbibing, lost his job.

If ever there was a city where a young, sensitive artist could be touched by a divine afflatus, it was Dublin at the turn of the century, a place and a time of cultural and political vibrancy, where everyone seemed to be striving to contribute to the great nationalistic movement reestablishing Irish language and tradition.

Colum gaelicized his name and joined the Gaelic League and the Irish Republican Army in 1901. The next year the publication of his prize-winning one-act play *The Saxon Shillin'* in his mentor Arthur Griffith's newspaper, *The United Irishman,* brought the young clerk to the attention of Yeats and the actor-directors William and Frank Fay, who wisely decided that the best way to teach stagecraft to a twenty-one-year-old neophyte playwright was to put him in a costume and on a stage. Colum first appeared as Buinne in AE's (George Russell) *Deirdre* when it opened on 2 April 1902 along with Yeats's *Cathleen ni Houlihan,* an evening in Molesworth Hall which Andrew Malone cites as the "real beginning of the Irish National Theatre."[2]

Other one-act plays Colum wrote during this apprenticeship period include *The Children of Lir* and *Brian Boru,* published in *The Irish Independent,* and *The Kingdom of the Young, The Foleys,* and *Eoghan's Wife,* published in *The United Irishman.* However, only *The Saxon Shillin'* stirred attention. It is the story of Frank Kearney, a young Irishman in the

British army, who, when he learns that the army expects him to help
evict his own family and destroy their home, seizes his father's gun
and, calling upon other Irishmen to take up arms, goes to his death.
The play's moral, uttered in the line, "We can't buy ourselves back
with the money we sold ourselves for," touched every Irish reader,
but it caused Willie Fay to renege on a production promised by the
Irish National Theatre Society for fear that the play would be considered inflammatory and be subject to censorship. *The Saxon Shillin'*
was performed, however, by an amateur group, the Daughters of
Erin, at the Bamba Hall on 15 May 1903.

The notoriety of *The Saxon Shillin'* provoked Colum into working
furiously on a full-length play to be called *Broken Soil,* the first of three
plays written for the Irish stage from 1903 to 1910 which earned him
a significant place in the history of Irish drama. *Broken Soil,* produced
on 3 December 1903 in Molesworth Hall, became a mainstay of the
newly formed Irish National Theatre Society. Colum was immediately identified as one of the big three of Irish drama along with Yeats
and John Millington Synge. If these three men did not share a community of vision, subject, or method, they did share a love for Ireland, a respect for their Irish roots, and a dedication to the new dramatic movement.

Colum extensively revised *Broken Soil* for a 1907 revival and re-
titled it *The Fiddler's House.* The revision is far superior to the original piece. The first title symbolizes the protagonist's break with the
life of a farmer to pursue music and the road, whereas the second
title pays homage to Ibsen's *A Doll's House;* from the very beginning
the young playwright, in contradistinction to Yeats, argued for an
Irish national drama based on the Norwegian's Model of Realism.[3]
When Colum left Ireland for America in 1914 with his wife, the critic
Mary Maguire Colum, he abandoned Ibsenism and Irish themes,
to his and Irish drama's great loss.

The Fiddler's House is the story of a middle-aged peasant fiddler,
Conn Hourican, who must choose between the romance of the road

and his duty to his children and the land. The play is an allegory on freedom, with the irresponsible, music-loving Conn representing one extreme and James Moynihan, the acquisitive son of a grasping farmer, the other. Conn returns to the road while his daughters finally settle on the land with young farmers suited to their individual personalities. The play's strength lies in characterization: Conn, the loveable, artistic ne'er-do-well; Maire, his devoted Antigone-like daughter willing to go on the road to be near her beloved father; and Brian, Maire's sexy, amoral lover, who wins her back.

The Land, produced in the Abbey Theatre on 9 June 1905, six months after it opened, was the first popular success the Abbey enjoyed, due in part to the great interest in the play's subject: the conflict in the younger generation between farming the land the older generation had fought for, or emigrating to America, the glittering land of opportunity beyond the sea. The scene is set at the turn of the century, following the long bitter "land war" and just after the passage of the Land Purchase Act, a reform law which allowed peasants to purchase the land they worked with money advanced by the government, provided both tenant and landlord agreed on the price. However, the reform had come about only after a long, bloody battle.

In *The Land* the victorious generation is represented by Murtagh Cosgar and Martin Douras, both sixty-year-old farmers who deeply love the soil they had struggled for. Douras had suffered imprisonment for the "cause," while Cosgar, in working his heart out, had driven away his embittered children, except for two: Sally, the vapid daughter, and Matt, the intelligent son. Martin Douras also has two children: Cornelius, a gentle, verbose fool, and Ellen, a young woman educated to the point that she does not want to marry a farmer and make her life on the hard land.

Cosgar and Douras represent those for whom possession of the land is everything: the fruit of a victorious struggle, the key to economic survival, and the hope of political freedom. The fact that these two men cannot comprehend the questioning of their values by the younger generation, and the lack of enthusiasm for agrarian life on the part of their children, constitutes the central conflict of the drama: the struggle between those who see life on the land as economic freedom and those that view suspiciously a life that may be akin to slavery. Using Renaissance comedy's convention of the two warring families, Colum laconically weaves a pattern of tension, humor, anxiety, and familial struggle.

The bright children, Ellen and Matt, are the hope for Ireland's future. Both nation and soil need their intelligence and integrity. They are in love, but, unfortunately, the grasping Cosgar places impediments in their path, and Ellen suffers from wanderlust, while Matt wants to marry her so much that he unconsciously transfers his submission to his father to Ellen's equally strong will. Too late, Cosgar relents, but Ellen and Matt leave for America. She cannot endure the thought of life without the crowds of American city life, and he cannot endure the thought of life without her.

The older generation has both won and lost: they won the land and lost the best of their progeny. Cornelius Weygandt draws Colum's moral: "Matt and Ellen, the fit and the strong, go to America. Cornelius and Sally, the hare-brained and the drudge, remain. Symbolic this is, of course, of the situation in Ireland to-day, or at least yesterday."[4]

Ellen and Matt, the real prizes, more valuable than the land, attract chief interest. In their complexities and cross purposes, in their passion for each other, and in their guilt toward their parents and their country reside Colum's objectivity and Ibsen-like detachment from pat solutions and unencumbered endings. The impartial playwright does not condemn Ellen's education, which may have incapacitated her for the role Ireland needs her to play, nor does he condemn her legitimate aspiration for what she perceives as a better life. Conversely, the couple that stays at home, Sally and Cornelius, are not glorified for their choice. Clearly, they have little imagination and can hardly see beyond the limits of their fences. Una Ellis-Fermor points out that the play "is a cross section of a living society . . . in which men do the right things the wrong way and there is no plain, cut-and-dried issue."[5] In fact all the major characters—Cosgar, Douras, Ellen, Matt, Sally, and Cornelius—are flawed by their weaknesses, and are naturalistically driven to their inevitable destinies by internal and external forces, social, political, psychological, and sexual, which are beyond their control. Thus the play approaches a drama of Naturalism and achieves a level of literary excellence that set a standard for subsequent Irish dramatists—what D. E. S. Maxwell calls a "documentary fidelity."[6]

Of the big three of the early Abbey playwrights, Yeats, Synge, and Colum, only the latter comes truly close to the language of the peasant speaker. Yeats's poetic diction is far removed from the language of the people and Synge's language is heightened and not true to a time or a place. Colum's plainer, circumstantial diction, with fewer figures of speech and a more discursive manner, is a more exact replication of the native diction of the Irish Midlands, the speech of the greater part of Ireland in Colum's youth and today. Colum instinctively knew that for a repressed people language can be a mode of symbolic action, even a replacement for disestablished national institutions. Indeed, language may be survival. And the poet and intellectual do not have a monopoly on the treasure store of language. Colum chooses the slow-witted Cornelius to express the pain and bewilderment of the Irish people at the loss of some of their best, using fluid Irish-English syntax and metaphor: "Aren't they foolish to be going away like that, father, and we at the mouth of the good times?" Even the fool can be inspired by love of the land to shout: "The nation, men of Ballykillduff, do you ever think of the Irish nation that is waiting all the time to be born?"

In subject matter as well as in language *The Land* and *The Fiddler's House* opened the theater to realistic peasant plays as Yeats's Classicism and Synge's Romanticism could not do, so that serious national problems could be discussed in the drama and the Abbey could become a forum for national social and political aspiration. *The Land,* Colum's most political play, does not glorify Ireland. Rather it implies that a maturing nation has a myriad of difficulties to overcome.

In 1907 Colum made one of the great mistakes of his life. Contumaciously, he broke with the Irish National Theatre Society in a dispute over Yeats's assuming dictatorial powers over the company. Colum was not alone, but the loss for him was of profound significance because he needed the counsel and experience of Yeats, Lady Gregory, and Frank Fay. At twenty-six he was too young and too green to stand alone. The Abbey world had nurtured the primitive artist and given him the time and scope to develop. Nevertheless, Colum turned to a maverick group, the Theatre of Ireland, which produced *The Fiddler's House* in the Rotunda on 21 March 1907. Next they put on Colum's weak verse play, *The Miracle of the Corn,* on 22 May 1908 in the rented Abbey Theatre. It is a heavily allegorical, overtly literary, morality piece, and it added nothing to Colum's reputation. In it a rich farmer's wife gives his produce to the poor. Instead of diminishing, the farmer's supply increases and he grows even wealthier. The good wife is elevated into both a Ceres-like fertility symbol and a bountiful Virgin Mother providing a miracle of plenty. The action of the play is deadly, and Colum quickly realized that he had deviated from his own precepts. He returned immediately to what he did best, writing realistic Irish drama.

His next play, *Thomas Muskerry,* is Colum's only pure tragedy. The Abbey accepted it even though Colum was no longer a member of the Society. It was produced on 5 May 1910 and would prove to be both his farewell piece for the young National Theatre Movement and his most controversial play. *Thomas Muskerry* is not set in the countryside, but in the small-town society and workhouse world he knew as a child. It is the mean world of the nineteenth-century petit bourgeoisie. Thomas Muskerry is the master of the Garrisowen Workhouse. Unlike most of the people around him, with the exception of the poorest of the paupers he has cared for, he is a decent, compassionate man, a little vainglorious and somewhat smug, but basically a good human being. At sixty he has busied himself with routine daily life and the authority of running the workhouse. Lear-like, he is sure of his place in the cosmos as he prepares for a dignified retirement on a promised pension. He is certain his daughter and her family, whom he has treated generously, will continue to respect him, and he expects the world will continue to defer to him as "the master."

However, the play is an unrelenting saga of humankind's cruelty to fellow human beings. Muskerry's daughter cares only for herself. His granddaughter has inherited her mother's rapaciousness. Having been cheated by a scoundrel who has run off to America, leaving him to pay off debts and shortages, Muskerry is forced prematurely to resign his position when his daughter refuses to help him meet the shortage by returning a gift of money. The granddaughter also denies her mother part of a promised dowry to help pay off the older woman's indebtedness. The hardheartedness is passed on.

Fate, as in Greek tragedy, has chosen Muskerry for an unforseen destiny. He ends up a desolate inmate of the workhouse he once ruled, but, *felix culpa,* his suffering provides some wisdom, understanding, and instruction before merciful death ends it. In *Thomas Muskerry* the twenty-nine-year-old Colum captured the dignity of the aged and the poor. He sensed the terror that could possess the old when they are bereft of economic security and must live precariously on the edge of existence.

Like Synge's *The Playboy of the Western World, Thomas Muskerry* provoked conflict. Colum too was attacked for seeming to defame the Irish character in his realistic portrayal of Irish life. For three years after the play was produced, *Sinn Fein,* the nationalistic periodical, published a series of articles entitled "Muskerryism," which alternately praised Colum for his Ibsen-like realism and damned him for supposedly pandering to an English audience. Colum counter-attacked: "I have never written an Irish play for an English audience. *Thomas*

Muskerry was written for an Irish audience. . . . I have given my play to an Irish theatre. They are at liberty to produce it in London, New York, Paris. . . . I assure you . . . that any play written by me for a non-Irish theatre will have no connection with Ireland."[7] Colum remained true to his word for over fifty years.

Before leaving Ireland Colum wrote two more one-act plays, *The Destruction of the Hostel,* a children's play written for St. Enda's School and produced on 5 February 1910; and his finest one-act drama, *Betrayal,* which he originally wrote in 1912 for Arthur Sinclair in the hope of an Abbey production, but the play was too inflammatory for either a Dublin or London production given the pre-World War I mood. Lady Gregory scotched plans for a production in favor of a play of her own, and Colum and his wife decided to visit America at the behest of an aunt of his living in Pittsburgh. They left Ireland in August 1914, just as World War I was breaking out. What began as a visit ended in permanent emigration. The economic opportunities in America for a young literary couple were far greater than those available in wartime Dublin. Furthermore, Colum did not want to aid the British war effort, and he believed he could further the cause of Irish independence as a propagandist in America. Also with the strained relationship with the Abbey, his chances for continued recognition as a playwright in Ireland were limited.

Colum took *Betrayal* with him to Pittsburgh. There the Carnegie School of Drama was producing Irish plays and Colum was paid to supervise the productions. *Betrayal* had its first performance at the Carnegie School in 1914. Because of its revolutionary message it became Colum's most frequently performed play, with subsequent productions in Dublin, New York, Jerusalem, and elsewhere.

Set in the inn of a country town in eighteenth-century Ireland, the play's themes of resistance to foreign tyranny and the betrayal by the cowardly, opportunistic young of the old values of loyalty to a cause and those who serve it, are as fresh as tomorrow's resistance movement anywhere. In *Betrayal* two brothers, Morgan and Gideon

Lefroy, representing British authority, want the reward posted for the names of those Irish who assassinated a British army sergeant. There is a crowd in the street below their room, and Gideon gets the idea of having someone from the crowd appear above, seeming to betray the killers. The pseudo-informer would be offered protection, and the mock betrayal might provoke exposure of the assassins.

Peg, the Ballad Singer, comes up to beg Morgan Lefroy to intercede with the British colonel to save her son, who has been condemned as a deserter from the British army. The people below mistakenly believe that she has betrayed her countrymen and so she picks up a dagger and kills Morgan. His death is of no avail to her, however, for the bellman announces that her son has betrayed the cause to save his own skin.

Peg is an heroic symbol of Old Ireland, a peasant woman full of compassion, conviction, and strength. Her Irish English with its poetic lilt contrasts with the prosaic, image-sparse English of the Lefroys, as when she speaks of raising her son: "No father to help in his rearing or to teach him a trade when he came to the time he could learn one. No one he could take pattern by or look up to." On the political, social, and linguistic levels *Betrayal* successfully captures the anger and dissatisfaction of many of the Irish people on the eve of the 1916 Easter Rebellion.

Betrayal was Colum's last play about Ireland until his Noh plays of the 1960s. In those plays he wrote for the Irish stage, Colum successfully engaged realistic drama, and sieved it through a poetic transformation so that it rose above what Yeats called the mere "sensation of an external reality."[8] Most significantly, his laconic style foreshadows more modernistic attitudes and methods culminating in the Spartan-like, sign-laden prose of Samuel Beckett and Harold Pinter. Simultaneously, his translation of common Irish speech to the theater and his use of Irish English syntax, inflections, and imagery led the way, along with Synge's musical, theatrically colored language, for the achievements of Sean O'Casey and Brendan Behan. Furthermore, although Yeats and Synge ultimately dominated the early history of modern Irish drama, Yeats failed to foster poetic drama and Synge's artificial dramatic rhetoric spawned few progeny, whereas Colum's straightforward, realistic theater of and for the people became the model for the mainstream of Irish drama in the twentieth century.

Lastly, but of great significance for the Irish people, Colum's early plays are of sociological and historical importance. They remain an evocation of a time gone and nearly forgotten except in a few works of literature, including Colum's epic novel *The Flying Swans* (1957). The plays now show the Irish people the world of their Victorian ancestors, with all the hopes, fears, misfortunes, and imperfections those struggling people had, and they present that view through the frame of the attitudes and aesthetic values of a seething, energetic Edwardian Ireland on the eve of the great struggle for independence.

However, even while still in Ireland, Colum, perhaps ill-advisedly, was searching for another set of dramatic criteria. He seemed to think that he was writing for an exclusively Irish audience and thus had parochialized himself. He sought universality, not realizing in his youth and inexperience that he had attained it. And so he began almost a lifetime of nearly fruitless and usually frustrating experimentation until he found his Irish dramatic voice again in the 1960s with his Noh plays.

In 1907 Colum wrote *The Desert,* a play he would revise and re-title several times over a fifty-year period. He incorrectly thought that a simple folk tale of a desert-wandering beggar who rises to power and then winds up back in the desert in his original condition could be the material for an epic drama. Colum mistook exoticism for profundity, and when the Dublin Gate Theatre finally gave the play two performances on 29 December 1931 and 7 January 1932, with the young Orson Welles portraying the King of Persia, the play was a resounding failure. Undaunted, the playwright revised and revised. Four surviving versions are set in such diverse places as North Africa, Baalbek in Lebanon, Persepolis in Persia, and Islamic West Africa.

The title migrated too, from *The Desert* to *Mogu the Wanderer* to *The Vizar* and finally to *Timbuktu*. The characters changed, and the first and last versions do not share a single piece of dialogue.

Another long-term drain on Colum's dramatic energies was his second non-Irish play, *Theodora of Byzantium*, first written in 1912. He continued to revise the piece for forty-five years, although it never was produced or published. In its "final" form it is titled *The Bear Keeper's Daughter* and is based on Procopius' history of Theodora and Justinian of Byzantium. Theodora is a well-drawn character torn between the Christian and pagan elements in her personality, and the play has several good moments, as when Theodora is involved in pagan rituals and when she helps thwart a plot to overthrow Justinian, but for the most part the script is a hodgepodge.

In 1917 in New York Colum collaborated with F. E. Washburn Freund in adapting Mrs. Freund's translation of Eduard Keyserling's *Ein Frühlingsopfer* (1899), recasting the German work as an Irish peasant play. As *The Grasshopper* it was first produced in April 1917 at the Garrick Theatre in New York. It was Colum's only Broadway production. The reviewer Louis Sherman noted: "The character drawing, the picture of Irish peasant life in the early part of the Nineteenth Century, the superstition, the vague spiritual yearnings, and the mysticism of the peasantry, all these elements are fascinating. But unfortunately not fascinating enough to overcome the effect of its verbosity and tedium."[9]

Unable to have the play performed again in America, Colum convinced Lennox Robinson to direct a production at the Abbey. There was one performance, on 24 October 1922, about which a reviewer said: "the play is pure Abbey Theatre of the earlier vintage, the period when Colum's 'The Land' and Synge's 'Well of the Saints' were first presented. . . . On the whole, 'Grasshopper' is a play of much merit and a credible addition to the Abbey list. There is a good deal of the early Colum in it — especially about the dialogue."[10] Unfortunately, the only known copy of the script was destroyed in the Abbey fire on 17 July 1951.

Colum wrote one more drama before starting on his Noh plays in the 1960s. *Balloon,* a fantasy drama in four acts, was published by Macmillan in 1929 and finally produced at the Ogunquit Playhouse in Maine, where it had a two-week run commencing 12 August 1946. Colum hoped and struggled for a Broadway production of *Balloon.* Typically, the play went through innumerable revisions. It never made it to New York. Colum called it "the most famous unproduced play on Broadway." As a result: "The usual disappointment. . . . So I am a foiled, frustrated playwright."[11]

Balloon is a highly imaginative, expressionistic quest for both a definition of the hero in modern society and a rejection of materialistic values in the hope of a return to a simpler life. It is set in and just outside "Megalopolis'" Hotel Daedalus. The hotel's name is one of several echoes of Joyce's *A Portrait of the Artist as a Young Man.* The play's hero, Caspar, earns a living tending a telescope in a park adjoining the hotel, where looking at the moon reminds him of the vastness and timelessness of the universe. Yet he craves a taste of the "good life" in the hotel on top of which is moored a giant balloon in which celebrities are to make an ascent in a publicity stunt. Like Stephen Daedalus, Caspar searches for truth and reality. After several adventures in the hotel, a metaphor for twentieth-century urban life, he finds his true love and comes to the realization that a hero is one who knows himself and who achieves what he is capable of achieving.

In a way *Balloon* is an urban version of *The Land* in respect to the play's central conflict: the temptation of worldly success and pleasure versus the value of a return to the older, slower ways of life in communion with the natural world. Unfortunately, the play's plot is improbable and the allegory too obvious and too heavy for the situation. Colum needed to abandon his dream of writing a "modern," universal, commercial play and return to his Irish background for inspiration and subject matter. Unfortunately, it would take him decades to realize this.

However, as Colum's reputation as a playwright waned and nearly disappeared, his renown as a lyric poet grew. His early verse, written under the tutelage of AE, found an appreciative Irish audience in *Wild Earth* (1907). In New York *Wild Earth and Other Poems* (1916) and *Dramatic Legends and Other Poems* (1922) brought his poetry to the full attention of the English-speaking world, and later on, three collected editions of his poetry, *Poems* (1932), *The Collected Poems of Padraic Colum* (1953) and *The Poet's Circuits: Collected Poems of Ireland* (1960), firmly established Colum's reputation as a major Irish poet of the twentieth century. He also made significant contributions with biographies of two friends: *Our Friend James Joyce* (1958) co-authored with Mary Colum, and *Ourselves Alone: The Story of Arthur Griffith and the Origin of the Irish Free State* (1959).

Mary Colum, Padraic Colum's beloved "Molly," the beautiful model for so many of the women in Colum's work, died in 1957, and Colum began again to concentrate artistically on his and Ireland's past. The amazing literary efforts of the last decade of his life, his eighties, resulted in the moving and exquisite final poems, *Images of Departure* (1969), and the Noh plays, which taken together are an epic Irish historical drama.

Colum's five Noh plays (1961–66) are his belated homage to Yeats, a recognition of the great poet's later dramatic aesthetic, the belief that the stage was ready for "the whole wealth of modern lyricism, for an art that is close to pure music, for those energies that would free the arts from imitation, that would ally art to decoration and to dance."[12] In regaining his Irish vision Colum abandoned the Ibsenism that has initially accompanied that vision. He accepted poetic drama with music and dance in place of stage realism, stark settings, and the verisimilitude of native speech. He would now attempt to forge "a complexity of rhythm, colour, gesture, not space pervading like the intellect, but a memory and a prophecy."[13]

Noh drama came to Irish drama from the Japanese tradition be-cause in 1915 Ezra Pound introduced it to Yeats, who latched onto it as he had done earlier with symbolist drama. Yeats singled out those elements of the form that coincided with his aesthetic, in this case the stylized movements of actor-dancers; the integration of words, dance, and costume; the mythic nature of character; and the use of masks. Noh makes heavy demands on the audience, requiring the ability to comprehend poetry and appreciate stylized action on several levels simultaneously. Instead of telling a story in the West-ern manner, Noh evokes emotional states or creates specific moods through retrospection. Traditionally, a Japanese Noh cycle contains five short, very different plays, combining poetry and prose: a play in praise of the gods, a warrior play, a play about women, a play about a living person, and a ghost play. Characters are few, costumes are elaborate, and settings are simple. Noh is probably the world's most controlled theater.

In addressing the challenge of Noh, Colum noted his methods and alterations: "I've attempted to modify the form of the Noh play. Yeats had done it before for the Irish theatre you know. But his con-tained purely legendary characters. . . . First of all it's a play that has [its setting] at a shrine where some extraordinary event happened . . . you can have changes in time. . . . How do you get the poetry in? How do you get spiritual life? That's the problem. . . . [I attempted to take] the Japanese form and use it in a new way, the ritual, the sound, and so on."[14]

As in the Japanese model Colum's Noh plays are a five-play cycle containing poetry and prose. Each is named after and located in an ancient place of significance in Irish history: *Moytura, Glendalough, Cloughoughter, Monasterboice,* and *Kilmore;* and each focuses on a nineteenth- or twentieth-century figure in Irish history or literature: Sir William Wilde, Charles Stewart Parnell, Roger Casement, James Joyce, and Henry Joy McCracken, whose personal crises are delib-erated as they relive the turning points of their lives in fictionalized association with the historic setting. Unlike the Japanese protagonists Colum's heroes do not find answers to their diffiulties; they only come to state and deliberate their dilemmas.

Of the five Noh plays only *Moytura* has been published before this selection. It also had a performance at the Dublin Festival in September 1963. Colum grouped *Glendalough, Cloughoughter,* and *Monasterboice* together as a three-act play, and they were performed as *The Challengers* at the Lantern Theatre in Dublin in February 1966.

In *Moytura,* which Colum subtitled "A Play for Dancers," the ghost of Sir William Wilde, Oscar Wilde's father, once a surgeon and a distinguished antiquarian, comes to the battleground of Moytura, where in prehistoric times the forces of light fought with the forces of darkness. Sir William had both forces within him. His agony is that at Moytura, which he had excavated and built his house on, he must relive the pain of the news that his two illegitimate, disowned daughters have been burned to death in an accident. Two choral figures in the background describe the violent emotions of ancient warriors as Wilde's emotions rise upon hearing the terrible news. Wilde speaks to the titan Nuada, an ancient Irish king, who gives him strength and comfort so that he can endure the awful guilt that plagues him even in death. In the epilogue another chorus figure offers judgment on Wilde, who, although exonerated by the court, was condemned by the public.

Colum implies, in *Moytura,* that history is not merely a continuum but is also the echoing memory of layers of past events. He successfully merges and blends the various historical periods in the play, in this the most Yeats-like and poetic of his Noh plays.

Glendalough, perhaps the most successful of the Noh plays, anatomizes the challenge of leadership when, as often happens both in life and in Colum's Noh plays, the people served betray their leader at the time he is in need of their support. The protagonist is the Irish patriot and statesman Charles Stewart Parnell, a charismatic and capable politician who was leading Ireland toward Home Rule in the

1880s by skillful maneuvering in the parliament in London. Parnell had a mistress, Kathleen O'Shea, wife of one of his supporters whose career Parnell had advanced. In 1889, the year of *Glendalough,* her husband, who seems to have known about the affair since its inception eight years before, sued Kathleen for divorce, charging adultery and naming Parnell as corespondent. The scandal ruined Parnell, destroyed his leadership, smashed the hopes of the Irish for Home Rule, and drove him to an early death in 1891 at the age of 45.

Glendalough takes place after the divorce but before a meeting of the Irish parliamentary party which would soon depose Parnell as leader. Realizing that the meeting will be the pivotal point of his life, Parnell comes to Glendalough, in County Wicklow, the site of a sixth-century monastery founded by St. Kevin and of a medieval university. Parnell is seeking self-revelation and inner understanding.

At Glendalough St. Kevin was tempted by Morrigu, the Great Queen, whom he threw down a cliff and into a lake because she wished to share his bed. Later she returned as the Hag of Glendalough, Kathleen. Parnell, no saint of course, in contrast to St. Kevin did not resist temptation. In succumbing he ruined himself, betrayed his people, and in return was betrayed by them.

Besides Parnell, the cast of *Glendalough* consists of his sister Anna, an emissary from the prime minister in London, two choruses, and four apparitions. The play relates the major events leading to Parnell's fall, including his helping his agent, Captain O'Shea, to win a seat in parliament; his hubristic refusal of ministerial aid; his victory and vindication in the Richard Pigott forgery case, in which he had been falsely accused of sedition; and the fateful reaction of Ireland's Catholic bishops to the divorce which led to his rejection by the Irish people, torn between their love of Parnell and their disgust at the immorality of a "Protestant libertine." The fact that he married Kathleen O'Shea immediately after her divorce assuaged them not at all.

Through skillful use of historical events and dialogue between

Parnell and his sister and two of the apparitions, the Hag and Pigott, Colum deftly reveals both Parnell's leadership qualities and character flaws. Colum is operating here on two levels: historical drama and character study. He has the hero face his mistakes and dishonesty, finally realizing that lust not only has destroyed him but also ruined a great force for Ireland's freedom. He realizes belatedly that he should have emulated St. Kevin, on whose church's ground he stands. Pigott's ghost rises up to remind Parnell of the forger within himself, but Parnell is able to realize that one day the Irish people will vindicate his honor, forgive his human frailty, and revere his memory for the love he bore them, the good he did them, and the great vision he had for them.

Glendalough works because of Colum's storytelling ability. Despite the complexity of the Noh form, the play captures the attention of the reader and presumably a theater audience because, regardless of how familiar they are with late nineteenth-century Irish history, they can relate to Parnell's personal tragedy, complete with tragic flaw, anagnorisis, catastrophe, and catharsis. As a Noh play, however, the central significance is that Parnell discovers the truth of his own nature. That is his solace and his consolation and the underlying theme of *Glendalough*.

Colum wrote *Cloughoughter* just before *Glendalough,* but he planned it as the third of the Noh plays, to follow the Parnell drama. The setting is the ruined castle keep Cloughoughter, which stands on a rock in Lough Oughter in County Cavan, where the great Irish warrior Owen Roe O'Neill died on 10 November 1649. As a youth he had fought in the battle of Kinsale in 1602, when his uncle, Hugh O'Neill, was defeated by Mountjoy, commander of Elizabeth I's army of occupation. But the protagonist of *Cloughoughter* is Colum's old warrior friend, Roger Casement, the revolutionary martyr who was executed by the British on 3 August 1916.

Casement comes to Cloughoughter before the rebellion to commune with the spirit of Owen Roe O'Neill, a man who had won victories over the English. He needs inspiration and he lacks confidence in his ability to lead the Irish Revolution. O'Neill and two veterans of Kinsale help Casement to decide to accept the leadership of the Irish cause. Finally, the fame that eluded O'Neill is won by Casement, as is stated in the epilogue in a ballad heard at Cloughoughter by Casement's brother after his execution.

Cloughoughter is extremely difficult to follow because of the use of two choruses and four entwining time levels: the early years of the twentieth century when Casement was at the height of his fame, Hugh O'Neill's time, the days of Owen Roe O'Neill, and the period following Casement's execution in 1916. Several passages of moving prose redeem the work however, as when Casement pledges that he will give his life for Ireland's honor, and his elegy: "And someday . . . look to the wee sails on the Western wave. The dreams of the dreamer live forever and mine shall surely be accomplished."

Monasterboice's protagonist is not a military figure but Ireland's greatest novelist, Colum's friend James Joyce, a culture hero whose battlefield is his inner self. His struggle is with the spiritual, cultural, and temporal powers of the Mother Church, from which compelling Jesuitical voices call Joyce back to belief, tradition, and obedience. He also struggles with the atavistic yet compelling grip of nationalism on young Irish men and women "who know that the fight is not for institutions but for the soul of a country."

As a youth fresh from the country Colum, the railway clerk, at first admired James Joyce, the dazzling university student, from afar. In 1903 they established a friendship that endured until Joyce's death in 1941. Colum tried to get Joyce published in Dublin, befriended his family, typed manuscripts for him, helped him financially, and finally wrote, along with Mary Colum, an affectionate biography, *Our Friend James Joyce. Monasterboice* is Colum's final tribute to his hero and beloved friend.

The play is set in the sixth-century monastery of the same name, where is located the great limestone Celtic cross within a circle, the

Cross of Muiredach, with figures representing the cycle of life carved on both sides. The shape of the monument, the cyclical nature of Joyce's work, and the cyclical structure of the play all merge into one visual, historical, and spiritual symbol.

Joyce comes to Monasterboice to find his own identity. He is accompanied by Emma Cleary, who is E. C. in *Portrait* and whose full name is used in the earlier work, *Stephen Hero*. Most of the play is a dialogue between Joyce and Emma, who tries to convince Joyce to marry, settle down, and return to the fold. The "emissaries," Jesuitical voices, urge Joyce to join them and remind us that the novelist's work is linked to Thomistic theory. Joyce rejects both the siren call and the appeal of a celibate life in the clergy. He goes off with his father and a crony for a "jollification" and then to a life of exile and greatness.

Colum links *Monasterboice* with *Glendalough* through the reintroduction of Morrigu the Great Queen, or the Hag of Glendalough, and through the recognition of Joyce's great respect for Parnell. Colum also uses *Monasterboice* to restate some of the central themes of Joyce's work and life: his rejection of the institutions of church and state, his view of marriage, his concept of art, and his personal sense of betrayal as symbolized by the treatment of Parnell.

Monasterboice is both more realistic and structually simpler than the preceding Noh plays and thus more easily comprehended, although it lacks some of the sense of history and tradition that the earlier plays display. Also Joyce's struggle for self-knowledge is not as intrinsically dramatic as the tragic experiences of Parnell and Casement. Still Colum knows Joyce better than his other Noh protagonists, and there are many fine moments in *Monasterboice*, when the words are as much Joyce's as Colum's, as when Joyce announces he is going "into exile. Into silence. Into cunning. *Non serviam*. Hawk that was driven here by the voice of the crowd, now show yourself to me."

Kilmore, written in 1965, marks the end of Colum's over sixty-year career as a dramatist. In the progress of his Noh plays Colum moved from the highly stylistic to the more realistic, with *Kilmore* the most realistic. Thus it offers excellent performance opportunities and more immediate audience appreciation, partly due to pageant-like qualities.

Kilmore is the place where Bishop Bedell once offered his protection to Irish Catholic scholars. There the Ulster leader Henry Joy McCracken, after vacillation and near betrayal of the Irish cause, makes the personal decision to continue the plans for the ill-fated rising of 1798 in the hope of uniting Catholic and Protestant Ireland, even though he knows that the promised support of a French landing will not be forthcoming and that the rebellion is doomed. The joining of Protestant and Catholic forces against England is reenacted in epic fashion. McCracken knows that in the end the sacrifice of the rebellion will "raise the spirits and pride of the Irish people."

Colum succeeds in his overall intentions for his Noh plays. They establish continuity between ancient and modern Ireland for viewers and readers. They retell history in thematic clusters, centering on pivotal historical and cultural figures. They examine the indecision and anguish of leadership as well as the painful choices artists have to make in serving their art. They successfully translate a non-European dramatic tradition to Western taste. Lastly, they proved to an old man who had always thought of himself as a dramatist that he still had those creative powers that had made him a meteor in the early days of the Irish Renaissance. The Noh plays have performances yet to come. In the end, as with his beautiful and moving poems of farewell, *Images of Departure* (1969), Colum returned to Irish themes. The Noh plays are proof and acknowledgment that the subjects and themes that worked best for him were always Irish ones.

In conclusion, Colum's production as a dramatist can be divided into three chronological periods. First is the pre-1914 years when he wrote his naturalistic, peasant plays, *Broken Soil, The Land, The Fiddler's House* revision of *Broken Soil,* and *Thomas Muskerry,* and when he penned his nationalistic one-act plays, the best of which are *The Saxon*

Shillin' and *Betrayal.* The 1914–1960 period was when he struggled in vain to find a commercial, international voice as he continually reworked *The Desert, Theodora of Byzantium,* and *Balloon.* Finally, in the 1960–65 period, he found his long-lost Irish dramatic voice and abandoned realistic theater. The greater contribution to theater history came early and was complete by 1910. For readers of Colum, however, discovery of the poetic intensity and the fine characterization of the Noh plays, as evidenced by the examples *Glendalough* and *Monasterboice,* will provide new, unexpected, and different aesthetic delights.

Padraic Colum died in a nursing home in Enfield, Connecticut, on 11 January 1972, a month after his ninetieth birthday. His body went home for interment in St. Fintan Cemetery, Sutton, County Dublin.

NOTES

1. Charles Burgess, "A Playwright and His Work," *Journal of Irish Literature,* 2, 1 (January 1973): 43.

2. *The Irish Drama* (London, 1929), p. 39.

3. *The Irish Independent,* 8 Dec. 1906, p. 4.

4. *Irish Plays and Playwrights* (London: Constable and Co., 1913), pp. 207–208.

5. *The Irish Dramatic Movement* (London: Methuen, 1939), pp. 188–89.

6. *Modern Irish Drama 1891–1980* (Cambridge, England: Cambridge University Press, 1984), p. 89.

7. Robert Hogan and Michael J. O'Neill eds., *Joseph Holloway's Abbey Theatre: A Selection from His Unpublished Journal* (Carbondale, Ill.: Southern Illinois University Press, 1967), p. 60.

8. Maxwell, *Modern Irish Drama,* p. 7.

9. "The New Play," *Globe* (NY), 9 April 1917, p. 17.

10. G. Hopper, "New Abbey Play: Young Actress's Success," *The Irish Times,* 25 Oct. 1922, p. 8.

11. As quoted in Zack Bowen, *Padraic Colum* (Carbondale, Ill.: Southern Illinois University Press, 1970), p. 18.

12. *Explorations* (London: Macmillan, 1962), p. 258.

13. *Ibid.*, p. 255.

14. As quoted in Bowen, "Ninety Years in Retrospect: Excerpts from Interviews with Padraic Colum," *Journal of Irish Literature* 2, 1 (January 1973): 31.

Selected Plays of Padraic Colum

THE LAND

An Agrarian Comedy
in Three Acts

CHARACTERS

MURTAGH COSGAR, a farmer
MATT, his son
SALLY, his daughter
MARTIN DOURAS, a farmer
CORNELIUS, his son
ELLEN, his daughter
A group of men
A group of boys and girls

SCENE: The Irish Midlands, turn of the century.

4

ACT I

The interior of MURTAGH COSGAR'S. *It is a large flagged kitchen with the entrance on the right. The dresser is below the entrance. There is a large fireplace in the back, and a room-door to the left of the fireplace; the harness-rack is between room-door and fireplace. The yard-door is on the left. The table is down from the room-door. There are benches around fire-place.*

It is the afternoon of a May day. SALLY COSGAR *is kneeling near the entrance chopping up cabbage-leaves with a kitchen-knife. She is a girl of twenty-five, dark, heavily-built, with the expression of a half-awakened creature. She is coarsely dressed, and has a sacking apron. She is quick at work, and rapid and impetuous in speech. She is talking to herself.*

SALLY. Oh, you may go on grunting, yourself and your litter, it won't put me a bit past my own time. You oul' black baste of a sow, sure I'm slaving to you all the spring. We'll be getting rid of yourself and your litter soon enough, and may the devil get you when we lose you. (CORNELIUS *comes to the door. He is a tall young man with a slight stoop. His manners are solemn, and his expression somewhat vacant.*)

CORNELIUS. Good morrow, Sally. May you have the good of the day. (*He comes in.*)

SALLY (*impetuously*). Ah, God reward you, Cornelius Douras, for coming in. I'm that busy keeping food to a sow and a litter of pigs that I couldn't get beyond the gate to see anyone.

CORNELIUS (*solemnly*). You're a good girl, Sally. You're not like some I know. There are girls in this parish who never put hands to a thing till evening, when the boys do be coming in. Then they begin to stir themselves the way they'll be thought busy and good about a house.

SALLY (*pleased, and beginning to chop again with renewed energy*). Oh,

5

it's true indeed for you, Cornelius. There are girls that be decking themselves, and sporting themselves, all day.

CORNELIUS. I may say that I come over to your father's, Murtagh Cosgar's house, this morning, thinking to meet the men.

SALLY. What men, Cornelius Douras?

CORNELIUS. Them that are going to meet the landlord's people with an offer for the land. We're not buying ourselves, unfortunately, but this is a great day—the day of the redemption, my father calls it—and I'd like to have some hand in the work if it was only to say a few words to the men.

SALLY. It's a wonder, Martin, your father, isn't on the one errand with you.

CORNELIUS. We came out together, but the priest stopped father and we on the road. Father Bartley wanted his advice, I suppose. Ah, it's a pity the men won't have someone like my father with them! He was in gaol for the cause. Besides, he's a well-discoursed man, and a reading man, and, moreover, a man with a classical knowledge of English, Latin, and the Hibernian vernacular. (MARTIN DOURAS *comes in. He is a man of about sixty, with a refined, scholarly look. His manner is subdued and nervous. He has a stoop, and is clean-shaven.*)

CORNELIUS. I was just telling Sally here what a great day it is, father.

MARTIN DOURAS. Ay, it's a great day, no matter what our own troubles may be. I should be going home again. (*He takes a newspaper out of his pocket, and leaves it on the table.*)

CORNELIUS. Wait for the men, father.

MARTIN DOURAS. Maybe they'll be here soon. Is Murtagh in, Sally? (CORNELIUS *takes the paper up, and begins to read it.*)

SALLY. He's down at the bottoms, Martin.

MARTIN DOURAS. He's going to Arvach Fair, maybe.

SALLY. He is in troth.

MARTIN DOURAS. I'll be asking him for a lift. He'll be going to the fair when he come back from the lawyer's, I suppose?

SALLY. Ay, he'll be going to-night. (*She gathers the chopped cabbage into her apron, and goes to the door.*)

SALLY (*at the door*). Cornelius! (CORNELIUS *puts down the paper, and goes to the door.* SALLY *goes out.*)

MARTIN DOURAS. Cornelius! (CORNELIUS *goes to* MARTIN.)

SALLY (*outside*). Cornelius, give me a hand with this. (CORNELIUS *turns again.*)

MARTIN DOURAS. Cornelius, I want to speak to you. (CORNELIUS *goes to him.*)

MARTIN DOURAS. There is something on my mind, Cornelius.

CORNELIUS. What is it, father?

MARTIN DOURAS. It's about our Ellen. Father Bartley gave me news for her. "I've heard of a school that'll suit Ellen," says he. "It's in the County Leitrim."

CORNELIUS. If it was in Dublin itself, Ellen is qualified to take it on. And won't it be grand to have one of our family teaching in a school?

MARTIN DOURAS (*with a sigh*). I wouldn't stand in her way, Cornelius; I wouldn't stand in her way. But won't it be a poor thing for an old man like me to have no one to discourse with in the long evenings? For when I'm talking with you, Cornelius, I feel like a boy who lends back all the marbles he's won, and plays again, just for the sake of the game.

CORNELIUS. We were in dread of Ellen going to America at one time, and then she went in for the school. Now Matt Cosgar may keep her from the school. Maybe we won't have to go further than this house to see Ellen.

MARTIN DOURAS. I'm hoping it'll be like that; but I'm in dread that Murtagh Cosgar will never agree to it. He's a hard man to deal with. Still Murtagh and myself will be on the long road to-night, and we might talk of it. I'm afeard of Ellen going.

CORNELIUS (*at the door*). It's herself that's coming here, father.

MARTIN DOURAS. Maybe she has heard the news and is coming

to tell us. (ELLEN *comes in. She has a shawl over her head which she lays aside. She is about twenty-five, slightly built, nervous, emotional.*)

ELLEN. Is it only ourselves that's here?

MARTIN DOURAS. Only ourselves. Did you get any news to bring you over, Ellen?

ELLEN. No news. It was the shine of the day that brought me out; and I was thinking, too, of the girls that are going to America in the morning, and that made me restless. (MARTIN *and* CORNELIUS *look significantly at each other.*)

MARTIN DOURAS. And did you see Matt, Ellen?

ELLEN. He was in the field and I coming up; but I did not wait for him, as I don't want people to see us together. (*Restlessly*) I don't know how I can come into this house, for it's always like Murtagh Cosgar. There's nothing of Matt in it at all. If Matt would come away. There are little labourers' houses by the side of the road. Many's the farmer's son became a labourer for the sake of a woman he cared for!

CORNELIUS. And are you not thinking about the school at all, Ellen?

ELLEN. I'll hear about it some time, I suppose.

MARTIN DOURAS. You're right to take it that way, Ellen. School doesn't mean scholarship now. Many's the time I'm telling Cornelius that a man farming the land, with a few books on his shelf and a few books in his head, has more of the scholar's life about him than the young fellows who do be teaching in schools and teaching in colleges.

CORNELIUS. That's all very well, father. School and scholarship isn't the one. But think of the word 'Constantinople'! I could leave off herding and digging every time I think on that word!

MARTIN DOURAS. Ah, it's a great word. A word like that would make you think for days. And there are many words like that.

ELLEN. It's not so much the long words that we've to learn and teach now. When will you be home, father? Will Cornelius be with you?

MARTIN DOURAS. Ellen, I have news for you. There's a school in Leitrim that Father Bartley can let you have.

ELLEN. In Leitrim! Did you tell Matt about it?

MARTIN DOURAS. I did not. (SALLY *is heard calling "Cornelius."* CORNELIUS *goes to the door.*)

CORNELIUS. Here's Matt now. The benefit of the day to you, Matt. (*He stands aside to let* MATT *enter.* MATT COSGAR *is a young peasant of about twenty-eight. He is handsome and well-built. He is dressed in a trousers, shirt, and coat, and has a felt hat on.* CORNELIUS *goes out.*)

MATT (*going to Ellen*). You're welcome, Ellen. Good morrow, Martin. It's a great day for the purchase, Martin.

MARTIN DOURAS. A great day, indeed, thank God.

MATT. Ah, it's a great thing to feel the ownership of the land, Martin.

MARTIN DOURAS. I don't doubt but it is.

MATT. Look at the young apple-trees, Ellen. Walking up this morning, I felt as glad of them as a young man would be glad of the sweetheart he saw coming towards him.

ELLEN. Ay, there's great gladness and shine in the day.

MATT. It seems to trouble you.

ELLEN. It does trouble me.

MATT. Why?

ELLEN. Everything seems to be saying, "There's something here, there's something going."

MATT. Ay, a day like this often makes you feel that way. It's a great day for the purchase though. Hom many years ought we to offer, Ellen? (MARTIN *goes out.*)

ELLEN. Twenty years, I suppose — (*suddenly*) Matt!

MATT. What is it, Ellen?

ELLEN. I have got an offer of a school in the County Leitrim.

MATT. I wish they'd wait, Ellen. I wish they'd wait till I had something to offer you.

ELLEN. I'm a long time waiting here, Matt.

MATT. Sure we're both young.

ELLEN. This is summer now. There will be autumn in a month or two. The year will have gone by without bringing me anything.

MATT. He'll be letting me have my own way soon, my father will.

ELLEN. Murtagh Cosgar never let a child of his have their own way.

MATT. When the land's bought out, he'll be easier to deal with.

ELLEN. When he owns the land, he'll never let a son of his marry a girl without land or fortune.

MATT. Ellen, Ellen, I'd lose house and land for you. Sure you know that, Ellen. My brothers and sisters took their freedom. They went from this house and away to the ends of the world. Maybe I don't differ from them so much. But I've put my work into the land, and I'm beginning to know the land. I won't lose it, Ellen. Neither will I lose you.

ELLEN. O Matt, what's the land after all? Do you ever think of America? The streets, the shops, the throngs?

MATT. The land is better than that when you come to know it, Ellen.

ELLEN. May be it is.

MATT. I've set my heart on a new house. Ay and he'll build one for us when he knows my mind.

ELLEN. Do you think he'd build a new house for us, Matt? I could settle down if we were by ourselves. Maybe it's true that there are things stirring and we could begin a new life, even here.

MATT. We can, Ellen, we can. Hush! father's without. (MARTIN DOURAS *and* MURTAGH COSGAR *are heard exchanging greetings. Then* MURTAGH comes in, MARTIN *behind him.* MURTAGH COSGAR *is about sixty. He is a hard, strong man, seldom-spoken, but with a flow of words and some satirical power. He is still powerful, mentally and physically. He is clean-shaven, and wears a sleeved waistcoat, heavy boots, felt hat. He goes towards* ELLEN.)

MURTAGH. Good-morrow to you. (*Turning to* MATT) When I get speaking to that Sally again, she'll remember what I say. Giving cabbage to the pigs, and all the bad potatoes in the house. And I had to get up in the clouds of the night to turn the cows out of the young meadow. No thought, no care about me. Let you take the harness outside and put a thong where there's a strain in it. (MURTAGH *goes to the fire.* MATT *goes to the harness-rack.* MARTIN DOURAS *and* ELLEN *are at the door.*)

MARTIN DOURAS. Ellen, I'll have news for you when I see you again. I've made up my mind to that.

ELLEN. Are you going to the fair, father?

MARTIN DOURAS. Ay, with Murtagh.

ELLEN. God be with you, father. (*She goes out.*)

MARTIN DOURAS. What purchase are you thinking of offering, Murtagh?

MURTAGH COSGAR. Twenty years.

MARTIN DOURAS. It's fair enough. Oh, it's a great day for the country, no matter what our own troubles may be. (MATT *has taken down the harness. He takes some of it up and goes out to yard.*)

MURTAGH COSGAR (*with some contempt*). It's a pity you haven't a share in the day after all.

MARTIN DOURAS. Ay, it's a pity indeed. (MURTAGH *goes to the door.*)

MURTAGH COSGAR (*with suppressed enthusiasm*). From this day out we're planted in the soil.

MARTIN DOURAS. Ay, we're planted in the soil.

MURTAGH COSGAR. God, it's a great day. (CORNELIUS *comes back.*)

CORNELIUS. This is a memorial occasion, Murtagh Cosgar, and I wish you the felicitations of it. I met the delegates coming in, and I put myself at the head of them. It's the day of the redemption, Murtagh Cosgar. (MURTAGH, *without speaking, goes up to the room left.*)

CORNELIUS. He's gone up to get the papers. Father, we must give the men understanding for this business. They must demand the mineral rights. Here they are. Men of Ballykillduff, I greet your entrance. (SIX MEN *enter discussing.*)

FIRST MAN. We'll leave it to Murtagh Cosgar. Murtagh Cosgar isn't a grazier or a shopkeeper.

SECOND MAN. It's the graziers and shopkeepers that are putting a business head on this.

THIRD MAN. If we're all on the one offer, we can settle it at the lawyer's.

FOURTH MAN. Sure it's settled for twenty years on the first-term rents.

FIFTH MAN. There are some here that would let it go as high as twenty-three.

SIXTH MAN. What does Murtagh Cosgar say?

SOME OF THE MEN. We'll take the word from him.

MARTIN DOURAS. He mentioned twenty years.

SECOND MAN. Not as a limit, surely?

OTHER MEN. We're not for any higher offer.

SECOND MAN. Well, men, this is all I have to say. If you can get it for twenty, take it, and my blessing with it. But I want to be dealing with the Government, and not with landlords and agents. To have a straight bargain between myself and the Government, I'd put it up to twenty-three, ay, up to twenty-five years' purchase.

THIRD MAN. More power to you, Councillor. There's some sense in that.

SIXTH MAN. I'm with the Councillor.

FIRST MAN. It's all very well for graziers and shopkeepers to talk, but what about the small farmer?

FOURTH MAN. The small farmer. That's the man that goes under.

FIFTH MAN (*knocking at the table*). Murtagh Cosgar! Murtagh Cosgar!

CORNELIUS. I tell you, men, that Murtagh Cosgar is in agreement with myself. Twenty years, I say, first term, no more. Let my father speak.

MARTIN DOURAS. There's a great deal to be said on both sides, men.

FIRST MAN. Here's Murtagh now.

MURTAGH COSGAR. Twenty years first term, that's what I agreed to.

SECOND MAN. And if they don't rise to that, Murtagh?

MURTAGH COSGAR. Let them wait. We can wait. I won't be going with you, men. I had a few words with the agent about the turbary this morning, and maybe you're better without me.

FIRST MAN. All right, Murtagh. We can wait.

FOURTH MAN. We know our own power now.

FIFTH MAN. Come on, men.

MURTAGH COSGAR. If they don't rise to it, bide a while. We can make a new offer.

SECOND MAN. We want to be settled by the Fall.

THIRD MAN. The Councillor is right. We must be settled by the Fall.

SIXTH MAN. A man who's a farmer only has little sense for a business like this.

SECOND MAN. We'll make the offer, Murtagh Cosgar, and bide a while. But we must be settled this side of the Fall.

SIXTH MAN. We'll offer twenty years first term.

MURTAGH COSGAR. Do, and God speed you.

CORNELIUS (*to the* MEN *going out*). I told you Murtagh Cosgar and myself are on the one offer. And Murtagh is right again when he says that you can bide your time. But make sure of the mineral rights, men; make sure of the mineral rights. (*The* MEN *go out;* CORNELIUS *follows them.*)

MURTAGH COSGAR (*with savage irony*). Musha, but that's a well-discoursed lad. It must be great to hear the two of you at it.

MARTIN DOURAS. God be good to Cornelius. There's little of the world's harm in the boy.

MURTAGH COSGAR. He and my Sally would make a great match of it. She's a bright one, too.

MARTIN DOURAS. Murtagh Cosgar, have you no feeling for your own flesh and blood?

MURTAGH COSGAR. Too much feeling maybe. (*He stands at the door in silence.*) (*With sudden enthusiasm*) Ah, but that's the sight to fill one's heart. Lands ploughed and spread. And all our own; all our own.

MARTIN DOURAS. All our own, ay. But we made a hard fight for them.

MURTAGH COSGAR. Ay.

MARTIN DOURAS. Them that come after us will never see them as we're seeing them now.

MURTAGH COSGAR (*turning round*). Them that come after us. Isn't that a great thought, Martin Douras? and isn't it a great thing that we're able to pass this land on to them, and it redeemed for ever? Ay, and their manhood spared the shame that our manhood knew. Standing in the rain with our hats off to let a landlord—ay, or a landlord's dog-boy—pass the way!

MARTIN DOURAS (*mournfully*). May it be our own generation that will be in it. Ay, but the young are going fast; the young are going fast.

MURTAGH COSGAR (*sternly*). Some of them are no loss.

MARTIN DOURAS. Ten of your own children went, Murtagh Cosgar.

MURTAGH COSGAR. I never think of them. When they went from my control, they went from me altogether. There's the more for Matt.

MARTIN DOURAS (*moistening his mouth, and beginning very nervously*). Ay, Matt. Matt's a good lad.

MURTAGH COSGAR. There's little fear of him leaving now.

MARTIN DOURAS (*nervously*). Maybe, maybe. But, mind you, Murtagh Cosgar, there are things—little things, mind you. Leastways, what we call little things. And, after all, who are we to judge whether a thing—

MURTAGH COSGAR. Is there anything on your mind, Martin Douras?

MARTIN DOURAS (*hurriedly*). No; oh, no. I was thinking—I was thinking, maybe you'd give me a lift towards Arvach, if you'd be going that way this night.

MURTAGH COSGAR. Ay, why not?

MARTIN DOURAS. And we could talk about the land, and about

Matt, too. Wouldn't it be a heartbreak if any of our children went —
because of a thing we might —

MURTAGH COSGAR (*fiercely*). What have you to say about Matt?

MARTIN DOURAS (*stammering*). Nothing, except in a — in what you
might call a general way. There's many a young man left house and
land for the sake of some woman, Murtagh Cosgar.

MURTAGH COSGAR. There's many a fool did it.

MARTIN DOURAS (*going to door*). Ay, maybe; maybe. I'll be going
now, Murtagh.

MURTAGH COSGAR. Stop! (*clutching him*). You know about Matt.
What woman is he thinking of?

MARTIN DOURAS (*frightened*). We'll talk about it again, Murtagh.
I said I'd be back.

MURTAGH COSGAR. We'll talk about it now. Who is she? What
name has she?

MARTIN DOURAS (*breaking from him and speaking with sudden dignity*).
It's a good name, Murtagh Cosgar; it's my own name.

MURTAGH COSGAR. Your daughter! Ellen! You're —

MARTIN DOURAS. Ay, a good name, and a good girl.

MURTAGH COSGAR. And do you think a son of mine would marry
a daughter of yours?

MARTIN DOURAS. What great difference is between us, after all?

MURTAGH COSGAR (*fiercely*). The daughter of a man who'd be sitting over his fire reading his paper, and the clouds above his potatoes, and the cows trampling his oats. (MARTIN *is beaten down.*) Do
you know me at all, Martin Douras? I came out of a little house by
the roadway and built my house on a hill. I had many children. Coming home in the long evenings, or kneeling still when the prayers
would be over, I'd have my dreams. A son in Aughnalee, a son in
Ballybrian, a son in Dunmore, a son of mine with a shop, a son of
mine saying Mass in Killnalee. And I have a living name — a name
in flesh and blood.

MARTIN DOURAS. God help you, Murtagh Cosgar.

MURTAGH COSGAR. But I've a son still. It's not your daughter he'll be marrying. (*He strides to the door and calls* MATT.)

MARTIN DOURAS (*going to him*). Murtagh Cosgar—for God's sake —we're both old men, Murtagh Cosgar.

MURTAGH COSGAR. You've read many stories, Martin Douras, and you know many endings. You'll see an ending now, and it will be a strong ending, and a sudden ending. (MATT *comes in.*)

MURTAGH COSGAR. You're wanted here.

MATT. I heard you call (*he sits on table*). So they're sticking to the twenty years.

MARTIN DOURAS (*eagerly*). Twenty years, Matt, and they'll get it for twenty. O, it's a great day for you both! Father and son, you come into a single inheritance. What the father wins the son wields.

MURTAGH COSGAR. What the father wins, the son wastes.

MATT. What's the talk of father and son?

MARTIN DOURAS. They're the one flesh and blood. There's no more strife between them than between the right hand and the left hand.

MURTAGH COSGAR (*to* MATT). We were talking about you. We were fixing a match for you.

MATT (*startled, looking at* MARTIN DOURAS). Fixing a match for me? (*He rises.*)

MURTAGH COSGAR. Ay, Matt. Don't you think it's time to be making a match for you?

MATT (*sullenly, going to the door*). Maybe it is. When you have chosen the woman, call. I'll be without.

MURTAGH COSGAR (*going to him*). We haven't chosen yet. But it won't be Martin Douras' daughter, anyhow.

MATT. Stop. You drove all your living children away, except Sally and myself. You think Sally and myself are the one sort.

MURTAGH COSGAR (*tauntingly*). Martin's daughter, Corney's sister. That's the girl for you!

MATT. We're not the one sort, I tell you. Martin Douras, isn't he a foolish old man that would drive all his children from him? What would his twenty years' purchase be to him then?

MURTAGH COSGAR. It wasn't for my children I worked. No, no; thank God; it wasn't for my children I worked. Go, if you will. I can be alone.

MARTIN DOURAS. O Murtagh, Murtagh, sure you know you can't be alone. We're two old men, Murtagh.

MURTAGH COSGAR. He daren't go.

MATT. Because I'm the last of them he thinks he can dare me like that.

MURTAGH COSGAR. There was more of my blood in the others.

MATT. Do you say that?

MARTIN DOURAS. Don't say it again. For God's sake, don't say it again, Murtagh.

MURTAGH COSGAR. I do say it again. Them who dared to go had more of my blood in them!

MATT. Ah, you have put me to it now, and I'm glad, glad. A little house, a bit of land. Do you think they could keep me here?

MURTAGH COSGAR (to MARTIN DOURAS). It's his own way he wants. I never had my own way. (To MATT) You're my last son. You're too young to know the hardship there was in rearing you.

MATT (exultantly). Your last son; that won't keep me here. I'm the last of my name, but that won't keep me here. I leave you your lands, your twenty years' purchase. Murtagh Cosgar, Murtagh Cosgar! isn't that a great name, Martin Douras—a name that's well planted, a name for generations? Isn't he a lucky man that has a name for generations? (He goes out.)

MURTAGH COSGAR. He can't go. How could he go and he the last of the name. Close the door, I say.

MARTIN DOURAS. He'll go to Ellen, surely. We'll lose both of them. Murtagh Cosgar, God comfort you and me.

MURTAGH COSGAR. Ellen; who's Ellen? Ay, that daughter of yours. Close the door, I say. (He sits down at fire-place. MARTIN DOURAS closes door and goes to him.)

CURTAIN

ACT II

Interior of MARTIN DOURAS'. *The entrance is at back left. There is a dresser against wall back; a table down from dresser; room-doors right and left. The fireplace is below the room-door right; there are stools and chairs about it. There is a little bookcase left of the dresser, and a mirror beside it. There are patriotic and religious pictures on the wall. There are cups and saucers on table, and a teapot beside fire. It is afternoon still.* ELLEN DOURAS *is near the fire reading.* CORNELIUS *comes in slowly.*

CORNELIUS. I left the men down the road a bit. We ought to take great pride out of this day, Ellen. Father did more than any of them to bring it about.

ELLEN. He suffered more than any of them. And it's little we'll get out of the day.

CORNELIUS. It's a great thing to have prophesied it, even. We'll be here to see a great change.

ELLEN. There will be no change to make things better!

CORNELIUS. Will you be taking that school, Ellen?

ELLEN. I'll wait a while. (SALLY *coming in; she is hurried.*)

SALLY (*breathlessly*). Oh, God save you, Cornelius. Tell me, is my father gone? I dread going back and he there! It was all over that baste of a sow that has kept me slaving all through the spring till I don't know whether greens or potatoes is the fittest for her!

CORNELIUS. He didn't go, Sally. I went down a bit of the road myself with the men.

SALLY. Oh, God help me! And I'll have to be going back to boil meal for her now. How are you, Ellen. (*She goes to* ELLEN.)

ELLEN. Sit down for a while, Sally; it's a long time since I was speaking to you. (SALLY *sits down beside* ELLEN.)

18

CORNELIUS. I'll leave this paper where they won't be looking for pipe-lights. There are things in that paper I'd like to be saving. (*He takes a newspaper out of his pocket and goes to room right*).

ELLEN (*to* SALLY, *who has been watching* CORNELIUS). Tell me, Sally, are they always that busy in your house? Is your father as harsh as they say?

SALLY. Father 'ud keep us all working. He's a powerful great man.

ELLEN. Matt will be bringing a wife into the house soon from all I hear. How would your father treat her?

SALLY. Oh, he'd have his way, and she'd have her way, I suppose.

ELLEN. And do you think your father will let him marry?

SALLY. Sure he must if the boy likes.

ELLEN. What would he say if Matt married a girl without a fortune?

SALLY. In my mother's country there are lots of girls with fortunes that Matt could have.

ELLEN. Supposing he wanted a girl that had no fortune?

SALLY. Oh, I suppose, father would give in in the end. It wouldn't be clay against flint when Matt and father would be to it.

ELLEN. You're a good girl, Sally. If I was Matt's wife, do you think you'd be fond of me?

SALLY. I'd like you as well as another, Ellen. (CORNELIUS *comes down from room.*)

CORNELIUS. I suppose they'll be here soon.

ELLEN. I have tea ready for them.

SALLY. Who's coming at all?

CORNELIUS. Some of the boys and girls that are for America. They are going to Gilroy's to-night, and are leaving from that in the morning. They are coming in to see Ellen on their way down.

SALLY. There are a good many going this flight. The land never troubles them in America, and they can wear fine clothes, and be as free as the larks over the bogs. It's a wonder you never thought of going, Ellen.

ELLEN. Father wouldn't like me to be far from him, and so I went in for the school instead.

SALLY. And now you've got a fine boy like Matt. It was lucky for you to be staying here.

ELLEN. Hush, Sally.

SALLY. Oh, I knew all about it before you talked to me at all. Matt always goes the the place where he thinks you'd be.

ELLEN (*rising*). I'll be in the room when the girls come, Cornelius. (*She goes into room left.*)

SALLY (*going to* CORNELIUS). God help us, but she's the silent creature. Isn't a wonder she's not filled with talk of him after seeing him to-day? But Ellen's right. We shouldn't be talking about men, nor thinking about them either; and that's the way to keep them on our hands on the long run. I'll be going myself. (*She goes towards door.*)

CORNELIUS (*going to her*). Don't be minding Ellen at all, Sally.

SALLY. Well, as high as she is, and as mighty as she is, she came into his own house to see Matt. God between us and harm, Cornelius, maybe they'll be saying I came into your house to see you.

CORNELIUS. Who'll know you came at all? And what isn't seen won't be spoken of.

SALLY. Would you like me to stay, Cornelius?

CORNELIUS. Ay, I would.

SALLY. Divil mind the sow. (*They sit down together.*)

SALLY (*after a pause*). Would you like me to knit you a pair of socks, Cornelius?

CORNELIUS. Oh, I would, Sally; I'd love to wear them.

SALLY. I'll knit them. We'll be getting rid of the sow to-night, maybe, and I'll have time after that.

CORNELIUS. And you come along the road when I'm herding. I don't want to be going near your father's house.

SALLY. O Cornelius, it won't be lucky for us when father hears about Ellen and Matt.

CORNELIUS. That's true. No man sees his house afire but looks to his rick.

SALLY. Come down a bit of the road with me, Cornelius. The sow will be grunting and grunting, reminding father that I'm away. Och, a minute ago I was as contented as if there was no land or pigs, or harsh words to trouble one. (*She goes to the door.*) The boys and girls for America are coming here.

CORNELIUS. Give me your hands to hold, Sally. (*She gives him her hands.*) We are as young as any of them after all. (*They hold each other's hands, then stand apart.*)

SALLY. It's a fine time for them to be going when the leaves are opening on the trees. (THREE BOYS *and* THREE GIRLS *enter. They are dressed for going away.*)

SALLY. God save you, girls. Good-bye, Cornelius. I'll have to run like a redshank. (SALLY *goes out.*)

CORNELIUS. I'll call Ellen down to you. (*He goes to the room door and calls.*) I'm going herding myself. Herding is pleasant when you have thoughts with you. (*He takes up the rod and goes out. The* GIRLS *begin whispering, then chattering.*)

FIRST GIRL. Sure I know. Every night I'm dreaming of the sea and the great towns. Streets and streets of houses, and every street as crowded as the road outside the chapel when the people do be coming from Mass.

FIRST BOY. I could watch the crowd in the street; I would think it better than any sight I ever knew.

SECOND GIRL. And the shops and the great houses.

SECOND BOY. There's no stir here. There's no fine clothes, nor fine manners, nor fine things to be seen.

THIRD BOY. There's no money. One could never get a shilling together here. In America there's money to have and to spend and to send home.

THIRD GIRL. Every girl gets married in America. (ELLEN *comes down.*)

ELLEN. I'm glad you came. I have tea ready for you. I can't go to Gilroy's to-night. (*Some come to the table and some remain near the door.*)

A GIRL (*at table, to* ELLEN). They say that a turf fire like that will seem very strange to us after America. Bridget wondered at it when she came back. "Do civilized people really cook at the like of them?" said she.

A BOY. It's the little houses with only three rooms in them that will seem strange. I'm beginning to wonder myself at their thatch and their mud walls.

ANOTHER GIRL. Houses in bogs and fields. It was a heartbreak trying to keep them as we'd like to keep them.

A GIRL AT DOOR. Ah, but I'll never forget Gortan and the little road to Aughnalee.

ANOTHER GIRL. I think I'll be lonesome for a long time. I'll be thinking on my brothers and sisters. I nursed and minded all the little ones.

FIRST BOY. A girl like you, Ellen, is foolish to be staying here.

SECOND BOY. She'll be coming in the Fall. We'll be glad to see you, Ellen.

ELLEN. I have no friends in America.

FIRST GIRL. I have no friends there, either. But I'll get on. You could get on better than any of us, Ellen.

SECOND GIRL. She's waiting for her school. It will be a little place by the side of a bog.

THIRD GIRL (*going to* ELLEN). There would be little change in that. And isn't it a life altogether different from this life that we have been longing for? To be doing other work, and to be meeting strange people. And instead of bare roads and market-towns, to be seeing streets, and crowds, and theatres.

ELLEN (*passionately*). O what do you know about streets and theatres? You have only heard of them. They are finer than anything you could say. They are finer than anything you could think of, after a story, when you'd be young.

A GIRL. You'll be going after all, Ellen.

ELLEN. I won't be going.

FIRST GIRL. Well, maybe you'll be down at Gilroy's. We must go now. (*The* GIRLS *go to the door.* ELLEN *goes with them.*)

ONE OF THE BOYS. Phil said that an egg was all he could touch while he was on the sea.

SECOND BOY. God help us, if that was all Phil could take.

THIRD BOY. Light your pipes now, and we'll go. (ELLEN *has parted with the* GIRLS. *The* BOYS *light their pipes at fire. They go to door, and shake hands with* ELLEN. *The* BOYS *go out.*)

ELLEN. Theatres! What do they know of theatres? And it's their like will be enjoying them. (SALLY *comes back. She is more hurried than before.*)

SALLY. Ellen! Ellen! I have wonders to tell. Where is Cornelius, at all? He's never here when you have wonders to tell.

ELLEN. What have you to tell?

SALLY. Oh, I don't know how I'll get it all out! Matt and father had an odious falling out, and it was about you. And Matt's going to America; and he's to bring you with him. And Cornelius was saying that if father found out about yourself and Matt—

ELLEN. Sally, Sally, take breath and tell it.

SALLY. Matt is going to America, like the others, and he's taking you with him.

ELLEN. Sally, Sally, is it the truth you're telling?

SALLY. It is the truth. Honest as day, it is the truth.

ELLEN. And I thought I'd be content with a new house. Now we can go away together. I can see what I longed to see. I have a chance of knowing what is in me. (*She takes* SALLY's *hands.*) It's great news you've brought me. No one ever brought me such news before. Take this little cross. You won't have a chance of getting fond of me after all. (*She wears a cross at her throat; she breaks the string, and gives it to* SALLY.)

SALLY. I don't know why I was so fervent to tell you. There's the stool before me that myself and Cornelius were sitting on, and he saying—(*She goes to the door.*) Here's Matt! Now we'll hear all about it.

ELLEN. So soon; so soon. (*She goes to the mirror. After a pause, turning to* SALLY.) Go down the road a bit, when he comes in. Sally, you have a simple mind; you might be saying a prayer that it will be for the best.

SALLY (*going to the door muttering*). Go down the road a bit! 'Deed and I will not till I know the whole ins and outs of it. Sure I'm as much concerned in it as herself! "No man sees his house afire but watches his rick," he was saying. Ah, there's few of them could think of as fine a thing as that. (MATT *comes in.*)

MATT. Well, Sally, were you home lately?

SALLY. I was—leastways as far as the door. Father and oul' Martin were discoorsing.

MATT. I've given them something to discoorse about. Maybe you'll be treated better from this day, Sally.

SALLY. O Matt, I'm sorry. (*She goes out.*)

MATT (*going to* ELLEN). It happened at last, Ellen; the height of the quarrel came.

ELLEN. It was bound to come. I knew it would come, Matt.

MATT. He was a foolish man to put shame on me after all I did for the land.

ELLEN. You had too much thought for the land.

MATT. I had in troth. The others went when there was less to be done. They could not stand him. Even the girls stole away.

ELLEN. There was the high spirit in the whole of you.

MATT. I showed it to him. "Stop," said I; "no more, or I fling lands and house and everything aside."

ELLEN. You said that.

MATT. Ay. "Your other children went for less," said I; "do you think there's no blood in me at all?"

ELLEN. What happened then?

MATT. "I'm your last son," I said; "keep your land and your twenty years' purchase. I'm with the others; and it's poor your land will leave you, and you without a son to bring down your name. A bit of land, a house," said I; "do you think these will keep me here?"

ELLEN. I knew they could not keep you here, Matt. You have broken from them at last; and now the world is before us. Think of all that is before us—the sea, and the ships, the strange life, and the great cities.

MATT. Ay—there before us—if we like.

ELLEN. Surely we like.

MATT. I was always shy of crowds. I'm simple, after all, Ellen, and have no thought beyond the land.

ELLEN. You said that house and land could not keep you. You told him you were going as your brothers went.

MATT. And I felt I was going. I frightened him. He'll be glad to see me back. It will be long before he treats me that way again.

ELLEN (*suddenly*). Matt!

MATT. What is it, Ellen?

ELLEN. I don't know—I was upset—thinking of the quarrel (*putting her hands on his shoulders*). My poor Matt. It was about me you quarrelled.

MATT. Ay, he spoke against you. I couldn't put up with that.

ELLEN. He does not know your high spirit. He does not know your strength.

MATT. Ellen, it's no shame for a man to have harsh words said to him when it's about a woman like you.

ELLEN. Let nothing come between us now. I saw you in the winter making drains and ditches, and it wet. It's a poor story, the life of a man on the land.

MATT. I had too much thought for the land.

ELLEN. You had. Have thought for me now. There is no one in fair or market but would notice me. I was never a favourite. I lived to myself. I did not give my love about. You have never offered me anything. In the song a man offers towns to his sweetheart. You can offer me the sights of great towns, and the fine manners, and the fine life.

MATT. Ellen! (*He draws a little away*). It's not me that could offer the like of that. I never had anything to my hand but a spade.

ELLEN. Your brothers—think of them.

MATT. They all left someone behind them. I am the last of my name.

ELLEN. Why should that keep you back?

MATT. His name is something to a man. Could you hear of your own name melting away without unease? And you are a woman. A man feels it more.

ELLEN. I do not understand men. Will you go back to your father's house after he shaming you out of it?

MATT. He'll be glad to see me back. He'll never cast it up to me that I went.

ELLEN. Matt, your father said words against me. Will you go to him and take his hand after that?

MATT. It was little he said against you. It was against your father he spoke.

ELLEN (*sinking down on a chair, and putting her hands before her face*). My God! After all my waiting, you talk like that.

MATT (*going to her*). Ellen, Ellen, tell me what I can do for you? There's land and houses to be had here. Father will let me have my own way after this.

ELLEN (*rising, with anger*). What does it matter to me whether he lets you have your own way or not? Do you think I could go into a farmer's house?

MATT. Ellen!

ELLEN. It's a bad hand I'd make of a farmer's house. I'm not the sort to be in one. I'm not like Sally.

MATT (*getting angry*). Don't be talking that way, Ellen Douras.

ELLEN (*with greater vehemence*). I must be talking like this. If you take me, you will have to go from your father's house. I always knew it. You ought to know it now, Matt Cosgar.

MATT. You didn't know it always. And you have let someone come between us when you talk like that.

ELLEN. I'm not one to be listening to what people say about you. Nor do I be talking in the markets about you.

MATT. I suppose not. You wouldn't have people think you gave any thought to me; I'm not good enough for you. The people you know are better.

ELLEN. You are foolish to be talking like that. You are foolish, I say.

MATT. I know I am foolish. Fit only to be working in drains and ditches in the winter. That's what you think.

ELLEN. Maybe it is.

MATT. Ellen Douras! Ellen Douras! A farmer's roof will be high enough for you some day.

ELLEN. May I never see the day. Go back, go back. Make it up with your father. Your father will be glad of a labourer.

MATT. Maybe you won't be glad if I go back; thinking on what you've said.

ELLEN. I said too much. We don't know each other at all. Go back. You have made your choice. (*She goes up to room left.*)

MATT. Very well, then. God above, am I to be treated everywhere like a heifer strayed into a patch of oats? Neither man nor woman will make me put up with this any longer. (*Going to door.*) When Ellen Douras wants me, she knows the place to send to. (*He stands at door. There is no sound from room. Going back he speaks loudly.*) I'll be waiting two days or three days to hear from Ellen Douras. (*There is no sound.* MATT *goes out. The room door is thrown open, and* ELLEN *comes down.*)

ELLEN (*furiously*). Two days or three days he'll wait for me. As if I'd go into Murtagh Cosgar's house. As if I'd go into any farmer's house. As if I'd get married at all, and the world before me. Two days or three days you'll wait. Maybe it's lonesome, weary years you'll be waiting, Matt Cosgar.

CURTAIN

ACT III

Interior of MURTAGH COSGAR'*s. It is towards sunset.* MURTAGH COSGAR *is standing before the door looking out.* MARTIN DOURAS *is sitting at the fire in an armchair.*

MARTIN DOURAS. It's getting late, Murtagh Cosgar.

MURTAGH COSGAR. Ay, it's getting late.

MARTIN DOURAS. It's time for me to be going home. I should be seeing Ellen. (*He rises.*)

MURTAGH COSGAR. Stay where you are (*turning round*). We're two old men, as you say. We should keep each other's company for a bit.

MARTIN DOURAS. I should be going home to see Ellen.

MURTAGH COSGAR. If she's going, you can't stay her. Let you keep here.

MARTIN DOURAS. She'll be wondering what happened to me.

MURTAGH COSGAR. Divil a bit it will trouble her. You're going to the fair anyway?

MARTIN DOURAS. I have no heart to be going into a fair.

MURTAGH COSGAR. It's myself used to have the great heart. Driving in on my own side-car, and looking down on the crowd of them. It's twenty years since I took a sup of drink. Oh, we'll have drinking to-morrow that will soften the oul' skin of you. You'll be singing songs about the Trojans to charm every baste in the fair.

MARTIN DOURAS. We're both old men, Murtagh Cosgar.

MURTAGH COSGAR. And is there any reason in your scholarship why oul' men should be dry men? Answer me that!

MARTIN DOURAS. I won't answer you at all, Murtagh Cosgar. There's no use in talking to you.

MURTAGH COSGAR. Put it down on a piece of paper that oul' men

28

should have light hearts when their care is gone from them. They should be like —

MARTIN DOURAS. There's nothing in the world like men with their rearing gone from them, and they old. (SALLY *comes to the door. She enters stealthily.*)

MURTAGH COSGAR. Ha, here's one of the clutch home. Well, did you see that brother of yours?

SALLY. I did. He'll be home soon, father.

MURTAGH COSGAR. What's that you say? Were you talking to him? Did he say he'd be home?

SALLY. I heard him say it, father.

MARTIN DOURAS. God bless you for the news, Sally.

MURTAGH COSGAR. How could he go and he the last of them? Sure it would be against nature. Where did you see him, Sally?

SALLY. At Martin Douras's, father.

MURTAGH COSGAR. It's that Ellen Douras that's putting him up to all this. Don't you be said by her, Sally.

SALLY. No, father.

MURTAGH COSGAR. You're a good girl, and if you haven't wit, you have sense. He'll be home soon, did you say?

SALLY. He was coming home. He went round the long way, I'm thinking. Ellen Douras was vexed with him, father. She isn't going either, Matt says, but I'm thinking you might as well try to keep a corncrake in the meadow for a whole winter, as to try to keep Ellen Douras in Aughnalee.

MURTAGH COSGAR. Make the place tidy for him to come into. He'll have no harsh words from me. (*He goes up to the room.*)

SALLY. Father's surely getting ould.

MARTIN DOURAS (*sitting down*). He's gone up to rest himself, God help him. Sally, *a stor,* I'm that fluttered, I dread going into my own house.

SALLY. I'll get ready now, and let you have a good supper before you go to the fair.

MARTIN DOURAS. Sit down near me, and let me hear everything, Sally. Was it Matt that told you, or were you talking to Ellen herself?

SALLY. O, indeed, I had a talk with Ellen, but she won't give much of her mind away. It was Matt that was telling me. "Indeed she's not going," said he, "and a smart young fellow like myself thinking of her. Ellen is too full of notions." Here's Matt himself. Father won't have a word to say to him. He's getting mild as he's getting ould, and maybe it's a fortune he'll be leaving to myself. (MATT *comes to the door. He enters.*)

MATT. Where is he? He's not gone to the fair so early?

SALLY. He's in the room.

MATT. Were you talking to him at all? Were you telling him you saw myself?

SALLY. I was telling him that you were coming back.

MATT. How did he take it?

SALLY. Very quiet. God help us all; I think father's losing his spirit.

MATT (*going to* MARTIN). Well, you see I've come back, Martin.

MARTIN DOURAS. Ay, you're a good lad. I always said you were a good lad.

MATT. How did father take it, Martin?

MARTIN DOURAS. Quietly, quietly, You saw Ellen?

MATT. Ay, I saw Ellen (*gloomily*). She shouldn't talk the way she talks, Martin. What she said keeps coming into my mind, and I'm troubled. God knows I've trouble enough on my head.

MARTIN DOURAS (*eagerly*). What did she say, Matt Cosgar?

MATT. It wasn't what she said. She has that school in her mind, I know.

MARTIN DOURAS. And is there anything to keep her here, Matt Cosgar?

MATT. I don't know that she thinks much of me now. We had a few words, but there's nothing in the world I put above Ellen Douras.

MARTIN DOURAS. I should be going to her.

MATT. Wait a bit, and I'll be going with you. Wait a bit. Let us talk it over. She wouldn't go from you, and you old.

MARTIN DOURAS. God forgive my age, if it would keep her here. Would I have my Ellen drawing turf, or minding a cow, or feeding pigs?

MATT. I'm fond of her, Martin. She couldn't go, and I so fond of her. What am I doing here? I should be making it up with her. What good will anything be if Ellen Douras goes? (*He turns to the door, then stops*). I came to settle with him. I mustn't be running about like a frightened child. (*The room-door opens, and* MURTAGH COSGAR *is seen.* SALLY *has hung a pot over the fire, and is cleaning the dishes at the dresser.*)

MURTAGH COSGAR (*at the room-door*). Sally, it's time to be putting on the meal. If you have any cabbage left, put it through the meal. (*To* MATT.) You put the thong in the harness?

MATT. I did (*pause*). Well, I've come back to you.

MURTAGH COSGAR. You're welcome. We were making ready for the fair.

MATT. I'll be going out again before nightfall.

MURTAGH COSGAR. I'll not be wanting you here, or at the fair.

MATT (*sullenly*). There's no good talking to me like that.

MURTAGH COSGAR. You said "I've come back," and I said, "you're welcome." You said, "I'm going out again," and I said, "I'll not be wanting you."

MATT. Father, have you no feeling for me at all?

MURTAGH COSGAR. Sure the wild raven on the tree has thought for her young.

MATT. Ay, but do you feel for me, and I standing here, trying to talk to you?

MURTAGH COSGAR. You're my son, and so I feel sorry for you; and you beginning to know your own foolishness. (*He turns to* SALLY.) I'm not taking the pigs. Put a fresh bedding under them tonight.

SALLY. I will, father.

MURTAGH COSGAR. Be up early, and let the cows along the road, or they'll be breaking into the young meadow.

SALLY. I'll do that, too.

MURTAGH COSGAR. Be sure to keep enough fresh milk for the young calf.

SALLY. I'll be sure to do it, father. (*She goes out.* MARTIN *takes out his paper, and begins to read it again.*)

MATT (*turning on* MURTAGH). Before I go out again there's something I want settled.

MURTAGH COSGAR. What is it you want?

MATT. Would you have me go, or would you have me stay?

MURTAGH COSGAR. Don't be talking of going or staying, and you the last of them.

MATT. But I will be talking of it. You must treat me differently if you want me to stay. You must treat me differently to the way you treat Sally.

MURTAGH COSGAR. You were always treated differently, Matt. In no house that ever I remember was there a boy treated as well as you are treated here.

MATT. The houses that you remember are different from the houses that are now. Will you have me go, or will you have me stay?

MURTAGH COSGAR. You're very threatening. I'd have you stay. For the sake of the name, I'd have you stay.

MATT. Let us take hands on it, then.

MURTAGH COSGAR. Wait, we'll see what you want first.

MATT. You have no feeling. I'd go out of this house, only I want to give you a chance.

MURTAGH COSGAR. Stop. We can have kindness in this. We needn't be beating each other down, like men at a fair.

MATT. We're not men at a fair. May God keep the kindness in our hearts. (MARTIN *rises.*)

MURTAGH COSGAR. Don't be going, Martin Douras.

MATT. Don't be going yet. I'll be with you, when you're going. (MARTIN *sits down.*)

MURTAGH COSGAR (*to* MATT). You'll be getting married, I suppose, if you stay?

MATT. Maybe I will.

MURTAGH COSGAR (*bitterly*). In the houses that are now, the young marry where they have a mind to. It's their own business, they say.

MATT. Maybe it is their own business. I'm going to marry Ellen Douras, if she'll have me.

MURTAGH COSGAR. Ellen is a good girl, and clever, I'm told. But I would not have you deal before you go into the fair.

MATT. I'm going to marry Ellen Douras.

MURTAGH COSGAR. Her father is here, and we can settle it now. What fortune will you be giving Ellen, Martin? That £100 that was saved while you were in Maryborough gaol? (MARTIN *shakes his head.*)

MATT (*stubbornly*). I'm going to marry Ellen Douras, with or without a fortune.

MURTAGH COSGAR (*passionately*). Boy, your father built this house. He got these lands together. He has a right to see that you and your generations are in the way of keeping them together.

MATT. I'll marry Ellen Douras, with or without a fortune.

MURTAGH COSGAR. Marry her, then. Marry Ellen Douras.

MATT. Now, Martin, we mustn't let an hour pass without going to her. (*He takes* MARTIN'*s arm, and they go to the door.*)

MURTAGH COSGAR. Marry Ellen Douras, I bid you. Break what I have built, scatter what I have put together. That is what all the young will be doing. (ELLEN DOURAS *comes to the door as* MATT *and* MARTIN *reach it.*)

MATT. Ellen! (*She shrinks back.*)

ELLEN. It's my father I came to speak to.

MURTAGH COSGAR (*going to the door, and drawing the bolt from the half-door*). When you come to my house, Ellen Douras, you are welcome within. (ELLEN *comes in.*)

ELLEN. It's right that I should speak to you all. Matt Cosgar, I am going from here.

MATT. Ellen, Ellen, don't be saying that. Don't be thinking of the few words between us. It's all over now. Father agrees to us marrying. Speak, father, and let her hear yourself say it.

ELLEN. I can't go into a farmer's house.

MATT. You said that out of passion. Don't keep your mind on it any longer.

ELLEN. It's true, it's true. I can't go into a farmer's house. This place is strange to me.

MATT. How can you talk like that? I'm always thinking of you.

ELLEN. I've stayed here long enough. I want my own way; I want to know the world.

MATT. If you go, how will I be living, day after day? The heart will be gone out of me.

MURTAGH COSGAR. You'll be owning the land, Matt Cosgar.

MATT (*passionately*). I've worked on the land all my days. Don't talk to me about it now. (ELLEN *goes to* MARTIN. MURTAGH *goes up to the door, and then turns and speaks.*)

MURTAGH COSGAR. Listen to me, Matt Cosgar; and you listen too, Ellen Douras. It's a new house you want maybe. This house was built for me and my generations; but I'll build a new house for you both. It's hard for a man to part with his land before the hour of his death; and it's hard for a man to break his lands; but I'll break them, and give a share of land to you.

ELLEN. You were never friendly to me; but you have the high spirit, and you deserve a better daughter than I would make. The land and house you offer would be a drag on me. (*She goes to the door.*)

MATT. Ellen, what he offers is nothing, after all; but I care for you. Sure you won't go from me like that?

ELLEN. Oh, can't you let me go? I care for you as much as I can care for anyone. But it's my freedom I want.

MATT. Then you're going surely?

ELLEN. I am. Good-bye. (*She goes out,* MARTIN *follows her.* MATT *stands dazed.* MURTAGH *closes the door, then goes and takes* MATT's *arm, and brings him down.*)

MURTAGH COSGAR. Be a man. We offered her everything, and she went. There's no knowing what the like of her wants. The men will be in soon, and we'll drink to the new ownership.

MATT. Oh, what's the good in talking about that now? If Ellen was here, we might be talking about it.

MURTAGH COSGAR. To-morrow you and me might go together. Ay, the bog behind the meadow is well drained by this, and we might put the plough over it. There will be a fine, deep soil in it, I'm thinking. Don't look that way, Matt, my son.

MATT. When I meet Ellen Douras again, it's not a farmer's house I'll be offering her, nor life in a country place.

MURTAGH COSGAR. No one could care for you as I care for you. I know the blood between us, and I know the thoughts I had as I saw each of you grow up. (MATT *moves to the door.*)

MURTAGH COSGAR. Where are you going?

MATT. To see the boys that are going away.

MURTAGH COSGAR. Wait till the Fall and I'll give you money to go and come back. Farrell Kavanagh often goes to America. You could go with him.

MATT. I'll go by myself, unless Ellen Douras comes now. The creamery owes me money for the carting, and I'll get it.

MURTAGH COSGAR. Then go. Good-bye to you, Matt Cosgar.

MATT. Good-bye to you. (*He goes out.* MURTAGH *stands, then moves about vaguely.*)

MURTAGH COSGAR. The floor swept, the hearth tidied. It's a queer end to it all. Twenty years I bid them offer. Twenty years, twenty years! (MARTIN *comes back.*)

MURTAGH COSGAR. The men will be coming back.

MARTIN DOURAS. I suppose they will.

MURTAGH COSGAR. You're a queer fellow, Martin Douras. You went to gaol for some meeting.

MARTIN DOURAS. Ay.

MURTAGH COSGAR. Them was the stirring times. I can't help but think of you in gaol, and by yourself. What brings you back now?

MARTIN DOURAS. Ellen told me to go back. I should say something to Matt, I think.

MURTAGH COSGAR. He went out as you came in.

MARTIN DOURAS. I'll go in when the house is quiet. I'll have a few prayers to be saying this night.

MURTAGH COSGAR. I'm going to the fair.

MARTIN DOURAS. I won't be going to the fair.

MURTAGH COSGAR. Why won't you be going to the fair? Didn't you ask me for a lift? You'll be going with me.

MARTIN DOURAS. I won't be going, and don't be overbearing me now, Murtagh Cosgar.

MURTAGH COSGAR. You will be going to the fair, if it was only to be showing that seemly face of yours. (*Going to the door, he calls "Sally!"*) (*He turns to* MARTIN DOURAS.) I've a daughter still, Martin Douras.

MARTIN DOURAS. You have, and I have a son.

MURTAGH COSGAR. What would you say to a match between them, Martin Douras?

MARTIN DOURAS. I have nothing to say again it.

MURTAGH COSGAR. Then a match it will be. (SALLY *comes in from yard.*)

SALLY. If you fed that baste on honey, she'd turn on you. Cabbage I gave her and got into trouble for it, and now she's gone and trampled the bad potatoes till they're hardly worth the boiling. I'll put the bush in the gap when I'm going out again, father.

MURTAGH COSGAR. Ay. Is that Cornelius Douras that's coming up the path?

SALLY. O faith it is. I'll get him to give me a hand with the trough. (CORNELIUS *comes in.*)

CORNELIUS. Well, Murtagh Cosgar, a great and memorial day is ended. May you live long to enjoy the fruits of it. Twenty years on the first term, and the land is ours and our children's. I met the men.

MURTAGH COSGAR. Ours and our children's, ay. We've been making a match between yourself and Sally.

CORNELIUS. Between me and Sally?

SALLY. Between Cornelius and myself?

MURTAGH COSGAR. Ay, shake hands on it now.

CORNELIUS. And tell me one thing, Murtagh Cosgar. Is it true that Matt's going to America, and that Ellen will wait for him for a year at the school? I met them together, and they told me that.

MURTAGH COSGAR. What they say is true, I'm sure. The land is yours and your children's.

SALLY (*wiping her hands in her apron*). O Cornelius.

CORNELIUS. Aren't they foolish to be going away like that, father, and we at the mouth of the good times? The men will be coming in soon, and you might say a few words. (MARTIN *shakes his head.*) Indeed you might, father; they'll expect it of you (MARTIN *shakes his head.* MURTAGH *and* SALLY *try to restrain him.*) "Men of Ballykillduff," you might say, "stay on the land, and you'll be saved body and soul; you'll be saved in the man and in the nation. The nation, men of Ballykillduff, do you ever think of it at all? Do you ever think of the Irish nation that is waiting all this time to be born?" (*He becomes more excited; he is seen to be struggling with words.*)

CURTAIN

THE BETRAYAL

CHARACTERS

GIDEON LEFROY, the keeper of an inn
MORGAN LEFROY, his brother—a magistrate
A BELLMAN
PEG, the ballad-singer

SCENE: An inn-room in an Irish country town.
TIME: Eighteenth century.

The scene is an inn-room in a country town. It was once of some fair degree of pretension and elegance, such as might be found in some old Georgian manor fallen into evil hands and ways. The principal feature is a large window in the centre up-stage wall. This window must be of sufficient size so that outsiders can look into the room and the audience can even be allowed to see a considerable part of the outlook as well. Several references in the text, such as "down there," can be explained by raising the outer floor a distance above the street level, and adding an outer vestibule and short flight of steps, as the action of the play absolutely precludes the usual outer hallway, and also the possibility that the room could be upon the second floor of the house.

The walls should be of plaster above the wainscoting, dull, grimy, dirty, and possibly cracked and broken as well. The woodwork, once white, would now be a dirty grey, or possibly even repainted into dirty yellow brown or light green; the furniture, odds and ends, rather sparse, old oak, and the curtains should be worn, faded brown or green. The window might also be shuttered. Finally, a general dusty and vacant air should pervade the interior, and the lights should be those of late afternoon or coming dusk. The entrance is at the back. Near the entrance is an upright desk. Before the window is a large table. At the back is a large sideboard.

MORGAN LEFROY, *a large, overbearing man, and his brother,* GIDEON LEFROY, *a meagre and dissatisfied-looking man, are in the room. They are regarding each other as if there were some conflict between them.*

MORGAN. Anyway, brother, I'll have my dinner here.

GIDEON. What will you have for your dinner?

MORGAN. What is there for dinner?

GIDEON. Salmon.

MORGAN. I had salmon at the bishop's yesterday, and salmon at Shirley's the day before. Is there nothing in this country but salmon?

GIDEON. There's nothing else in this house, Morgan.

41

MORGAN. Very well, my good brother. Let me have your salmon. (*He sits at desk. He takes out a deck of cards and lays them before him.*)

GIDEON. You must be at the cards, brother Morgan.

MORGAN. You had to be once, brother Gideon.

GIDEON. I can keep my hands off the cards now. (*Outside the* BELL-MAN'*s voice and bell are heard.*)

BELLMAN. Five hundred pounds reward. Five hundred pounds reward will be given to the person or persons who will give such information as will lead to the committal of the person or persons who murdered Isaac Hackman, Sergeant in His Majesty's Army.

MORGAN. Five hundred pounds reward! Five hundred pounds reward! And no way to come by it.

GIDEON. Ah, if you could only get the reward into your hands, Morgan!

MORGAN. Your fingers, I am sure, are itching for it.

GIDEON. No more than your own, brother Morgan.

MORGAN. It's a pity we can't come to it. (*The steps of the* BELLMAN *have been heard approaching. He comes to the door of the room ringing his bell. He comes in. He is fantastically attired, wearing the red, torn coat of a soldier, and with straw wrapped around his bare legs.*)

BELLMAN. Five hundred pounds reward — for information — that will lead to the strangulation — of the person or persons who sent to damnation — Isaac Hackman — a sergeant by persuasion.

MORGAN. Your place is in the street, my man.

BELLMAN. A salmon I bear — with all my care — for Gideon Lefroy, his honour there. (*He shows a salmon wrapped in straw.*)

GIDEON. Leave it there. (*The* BELLMAN *puts the salmon down.*) Who sent you with this?

BELLMAN. A man over there — the fish made me bear.

MORGAN. I suppose he would not come in here himself when he saw that I was here.

BELLMAN. As far as I know — he would not go — when your honour was seen in the street below.

MORGAN. The people outside might think you were informing on them, eh?

BELLMAN (*at the door*). You may drain the rivers and drag the ponds — but it's a man under bonds will put a man under bonds.

MORGAN. Come back, my man.

BELLMAN. My errand's rendered, and my duty's tendered. (*He goes out.*)

MORGAN. "The man under bonds will put another under bonds." Had he any meaning in that, Gideon?

GIDEON. No meaning at all. It's a way they have of talking. They're always saying rhymes out of old ballads.

MORGAN. Well, Maunders might as well keep the shilling that he is paying the Bellman. The town is filled with people, but there isn't one of them that would tell who murdered the Government agent — no, not for five times five hundred pounds reward.

GIDEON. That's true. Not one of them would tell. It's their religion, you might say, not to inform on one another.

MORGAN. And so neither you nor I nor anyone else will get that five hundred pounds. I wish to Heaven I could get some of it into my hands.

GIDEON (*with an excitement that is mastering him*). I have a way, Morgan.

MORGAN. A way of what?

GIDEON. Of getting the five hundred pounds reward.

MORGAN. What's the way? Speak out and let us hear it. Has a notion come into that narrow head of yours? Well, what's the way?

GIDEON. It is a way, I tell you. Listen, Morgan. Suppose we could get some one in the street below to come up here; suppose one of us talked to him in full view of the crowd, he not thinking of the crowd at the time. . . . Oh, but we can't get it done!

MORGAN. Go on, go on, Gideon.

GIDEON. Wouldn't they think that he was telling one of us who killed Isaac Hackman? Wouldn't they be sure to kill him when he went down amongst them? Wouldn't he know that they would be for killing him, and then . . .

MORGAN. What then?

GIDEON. Wouldn't he tell us everything—everything for the protection we could give him?

MORGAN. We could well give them the chance of seeing what's happening here. I suppose it was this gave you the idea—standing at this window and watching the street below the last day that the fair was here?

GIDEON. No, that's not the way it came into my mind. I was sitting at this table and the curtain of the window was open. A drunken peasant came up to talk to me about business. We sat down here, and were talking for a while. Suddenly the man's face went white as death. "They're watching us," he said. There was a throng at the blacksmith's forge over the way, and they were all looking into the room. I knew what the crowd had in its mind.

MORGAN. They thought that the fellow talking with you was betraying the man who murdered Isaac Hackman, eh?

GIDEON. That was it. "By my soul," said the fellow, "I was nearly turning the hands of the people against me. If it was Morgan Lefroy I was facing, I'd never leave the town alive." Well, I may say that that was what put the notion into my mind. Next day I thought it clean out.

MORGAN. Yes, it is a plan, and a good plan. Here's a room with a wide window to it. Anyone who comes here when the shutters are open must be seen by the crowd below.

GIDEON. If we could get one of them to come up here and talk to yourself privately! Every one in the fair would have their eyes on the two of you. The word would go round that the person with you was giving away the names of them that were concerned in the murder of Isaac Hackman.

MORGAN. And we know what would happen then, Gideon.

GIDEON. The people, I tell you, would become like maddened cattle. A woman would think that her brother, or son, or husband was being betrayed. God help the person that was here when they'd go down amongst the people.

MORGAN. They'd need a company of soldiers to protect them, and to get that they'd have to turn to us.

GIDEON. And we'd give them protection on condition that they gave us the names of those concerned in the murder of Isaac Hackman.

MORGAN. Ah, it's a masterly notion, brother Gideon.

GIDEON (*flattered*). If I was out of the bogs of Connaught I might make something of myself.

MORGAN. Yes, if you were in Dublin you might be sure of a Government post.

GIDEON. This affair might bring me into notice.

MORGAN. It might. Well, if we carry it through how much of the reward will you claim?

GIDEON. Half the five hundred pounds reward.

MORGAN. I'll give you an agent's commission.

GIDEON. That wouldn't be enough for me, brother Morgan. It was I and not you who thought of the plan.

MORGAN. That's so, that's so, brother Gideon. But you by yourself could never carry the plan out. It needs a man like me — it needs a man with the presence and the reputation of Morgan Lefroy to carry that business through. I'll play a game of cards with you. If you win — I'll make it halves.

GIDEON. I'm not like you — I can keep my hands off the cards.

MORGAN. I dare say. But then it's only a fellow like me — a fellow that takes chances and that likes taking chances — who could handle that scheme of yours. I gambled away my sinecure in Dublin Castle, and the rage for gambling hasn't abated in me.

GIDEON. Your winnings in this place won't make you popular — I'll tell you that, brother Morgan. Young Shirley came in here this morning to leave something you had won from him.

MORGAN. And did he leave it here? (GIDEON *goes to sideboard. He takes out a sword-stick from lower part of it. He brings it to* MORGAN, *who takes it and examines it with relish.*)

MORGAN. This is the sword-stick that he made such a swagger with. (*He unscrews it.*) The blade is Spanish steel. (*He leaves it on desk.*) It came to our pledging the things we boasted of—his sword-stick and my brace of bloodhounds. Now I have the sword-stick. (*As he lays out the cards* GIDEON *is drawn to the desk almost as hypnotized. He takes up the cards that* MORGAN *deals out.*)

MORGAN (*flattering* GIDEON). As you were saying, Gideon, this affair might bring you into notice.

GIDEON. It should. There isn't one here that knows these people but myself—not one. Maunders with his shilling Bellman! Much good it will do to send that fellow through the fair!

MORGAN. No good, no good at all!

GIDEON. Maunders doesn't know them. And look at the place the Government has given him!

MORGAN. Ah, if it weren't for our scheme, brother Gideon—

GIDEON. My scheme, Morgan, my scheme.

MORGAN. So it is. It's your scheme. Aye, it's a masterly notion, brother Gideon. Did you play?

GIDEON. There's my card. (GIDEON *wins. They play again.*)

MORGAN. And there's mine. That leaves me winners, I think.

GIDEON (*scrutinizing cards*). Aye, that leaves you winners.

MORGAN (*rising*). Bring me the brandy. (GIDEON *goes to sideboard, and brings bottle and glasses.* MORGAN *pours out liquor.*)

MORGAN. The usual toasts! There's to the pious, glorious, and immortal memory of King William the Third! (*He drinks.*)

GIDEON. How much am I to get?

MORGAN. An agent's commission, I said.

GIDEON. And how much might your agent's commission be?

MORGAN. Fifty pounds.

GIDEON. Fifty pounds isn't enough. My notion is worth more than that.

MORGAN. I save you all the trouble and all the danger — the danger, mind you — of working your notion out.

GIDEON. Very well, then. Let us say fifty pounds for the notion. How much for the rest?

MORGAN. What are you talking about?

GIDEON. You can have my notion for fifty pounds, but you can't have anything else, brother Morgan.

MORGAN. What else can't I have? Your goodwill, eh?

GIDEON. You can't have this room, for one thing.

MORGAN. I think, brother Gideon, that you think you can play with me.

GIDEON. And do you think you can play with me? The people outside are no friends of mine. They don't give me much of their custom. But I have to live amongst them, and it wouldn't serve me if my house had the name you would put on it.

MORGAN. Gideon, you cur, don't you know that I, as magistrate, could quarter a company of soldiers on you that would eat you bare as bones?

GIDEON. Could the like of that be done on a loyal man?

MORGAN. It could, and I'm the man to have it done.

GIDEON. Very well, then. You can have what you want. But what are we talking about, anyway? None of the men in the street will come up in this room when they know that you are in the place.

MORGAN. I have luck, I tell you, I have luck. (*There is a knock at the door.*)

GIDEON. It must be some one from the street. No one else knocks.

MORGAN. Open the door, Gideon.

GIDEON. Your luck is not for to-day, Morgan.

MORGAN. Open the door. (GIDEON *opens the door. A* WOMAN *of about sixty is seen waiting there. She is barefooted, and she wears the enveloping cloak that women in parts of Connaught still wear. She is agitated, but there is something stately in her bearing.*)

GIDEON. Who are you?

PEG. They call me Peg the Ballad-singer.

GIDEON. What have you come here for?

PEG. To speak with his honour, Mr Morgan Lefroy.

MORGAN. And what can I do for you, Peg the Ballad-singer?

PEG. I ran beside your horse when your honour was going to a meeting of the magistrates, and your honour made a promise to me.

MORGAN. And what promise did I make to you?

PEG. Your honour promised that you would see me in this place and on this day.

MORGAN. I did, eh? That's something I hadn't thought of. Well, here I am. Here I am and here you are, Peg. (*He makes a motion indicating the whole of the room.*) And I'll talk to you here, and I'll listen to what you have to say.

PEG. Your honour's over-good to a poor woman.

MORGAN. Do you hear what she says, Gideon?

GIDEON (*at the table beside him*). You'll be brought down, you'll be brought down, Morgan. (*He drinks brandy from glass and bottle left on table.*)

MORGAN. Dinner in an hour, Gideon. And mind how you treat me. It will be to your peril if you do not serve me to my liking. But first go down and give the people outside the messages that I spoke to you about before, the messages that I want delivered to them. (GIDEON *drinks more brandy, then goes out of door. His voice is heard speaking, as* MORGAN *opens shutters of window and stands in view of the people outside.*)

GIDEON'S VOICE. Mr Morgan Lefroy is here, and he bids me tell the people from Nobber that he is making a new avenue to his house, and he orders the people to send round horses and men for the work, as is their duty.

MORGAN. An old woman out there says that hell gapes for me. I know her. She always says that. And just because her son was amongst the batch I got transported. (*From the moment of the* WOMAN'S *entrance* MORGAN LEFROY'S *manner has changed; he is no longer violent; he is alert and careful.*)

MORGAN (*to* PEG). Well, here I am, my good woman. And what have you to say to me?

PEG. My son! I come to you about my son.

MORGAN. And what do you want me to do about your son?

PEG. My son is in gaol. Oh, if your honour will not speak for him, he will be shot down to-morrow or the day after!

MORGAN. And why will your son be shot down?

PEG. First he listed, and then he ran away from the soldiers.

MORGAN. He deserted, is that what he did? Deserted from the King's Army?

PEG. You might say that, your honour.

MORGAN. And you want me to do something for him?

PEG. To write a letter to the Colonel for him, for my son Terence. Oh, if your honour would only do that!

MORGAN. Is there anyone who would speak for him?

PEG (*eagerly*). Outside, it is, your honour?

MORGAN. Aye, outside. (PEG *goes to the window.*)

PEG. There's a crowd at the blacksmith's forge, and every one in it could speak for him and for me.

MORGAN. Give me their names.

PEG. Is it the names of the people outside, the people who would speak for my son and myself?

MORGAN. Aye. Give me their names. The names! I will write them down. For the letter that I am to send to Colonel Maunders.

PEG. There's Mainey Kelly, Cormac Farragher, Shaun O'Gorman, Hugh O'Keefe. (*She turns, and notices the way he is watching her.*) Oh, your honour, sure you intend no harm to me?

MORGAN. No, no. What harm could I mean for you? Give me the names again, and I will write them down. Else there will be no use in your taking this letter to Colonel Maunders.

PEG. Mainey Kelly, Cormac Farragher, Shaun O'Gorman. A woman has gone down on her knees. It's Mary Sullivan. She is praying that I may win the life of my son.

MORGAN. Let that be as it may. I have the names down that you gave me. And now I want to ask you something.

PEG. What is it, your honour?

MORGAN. You know everything that the people outside know?

PEG. I do, your honour. And more than they know. More, more!

MORGAN. What more do you know?

PEG. Something that was handed down to me by my father, and from his father's father.

MORGAN. And what is that?

PEG. The knowledge that there was once learning in Nobber, and the way of showing that there was.

MORGAN. Learning! In Nobber! Well, well. Why didn't they take the trouble of handing you down knowledge of something that was worth while?

PEG. Your honour wouldn't care about the learning that the people had, why would you? But my father and his father's father cared about it. There were books in their keeping. And when the last book was gone my father made me learn—

MORGAN. I hope it was a way to come to hidden gold.

PEG. No, your honour. Nothing like that. Only an old ancient poem that was made by a queen in the old days in Ireland.

MORGAN. You can say it for me. Come, let me hear it.

PEG. Queen Gormlai was her name, and, like many another, she came to poverty.

MORGAN. Stand this way and say it for me. (*He motions* PEG *to come to a place where she can be seen from the street. At first* PEG *speaks the verse diffidently. Then the situation in the poem dominates her and controls her agitation.*)

PEG. The Queen said:

> "Unseemly is the rag
> That's for my back to-day:

Patched and double-patched —
　　The hodden on the grey.
　　· · · · · · · ·
Here, here, I am begrudged
　　Even the candle's light
To put it on, the garb
　　That leaves me misbedight.

O skinflint woman, Mor,
　　Who knows that I speak true —
I had women once —
　　A queen's retinue!

Light of hand and apt,
　　And companionable:
Seven score women, Mor,
　　I had at my call.
　　· · · · · · · ·
Now this old clout to wear,
　　With root-like stitches through —
Not hands that worked for queens,
　　Nor fine things felt made you!

The bramble is no friend,
　　It pulls at me and drags;
This thorny ground is mine,
　　Where briers tear my rags!"

MORGAN. So that is what was given to you to remember?

PEG. To show that there was once learning in Nobber, your honour.

MORGAN. Well, there was an old poem handed down to me too, from my father and my father's father:

> "There was an old prophecy found in a bog,
>   Lillubollero O!
> There was an old prophecy found in a bog,
> That Ireland would be ruled by an ass and a dog,
>   Lillubollero O!"

(*At these words from the song of a dominating party* PEG THE BALLAD-SINGER *bends her knees.*)

MORGAN. I know no more of it than that. Well, we'll get to our business. So the people outside will speak for you, eh? For you and your son?

PEG. They will, your honour, and be glad to do it, and they would be proud that their words were taken by your honour.

MORGAN (*at the window*). But they are all looking at you very strangely, Peg.

PEG. Is the sight of a woman begging for the life of the one nearest to her so strange to them?

MORGAN. That woman is not praying—she is cursing.

PEG. And there's another woman on her knees. God help me that has to beg my son's life from a man cursed by the people!

MORGAN. You think that it is me that they are cursing. You are mistaken. It is you that the people outside are cursing.

PEG. Me! But how can that be?

MORGAN. I don't know what has happened. But I know that you daren't go out amongst them now.

PEG. What happened? What happened to make them like this?

MORGAN. I know. I know now what has happened.

PEG. Tell me. Oh, your honour, tell me!

MORGAN. This is it. Seeing you with me, seeing you talking to me so familiarly, they think . . . Blood and 'ouns! Don't you know what they think?

PEG. No, no, your honour. Tell me!

MORGAN. They think—and how easy it is for them to think it—
they think that you have been giving me the names of those who
killed Isaac Hackman!

PEG. My God, my God! (*She goes to the window as if to address fran-
tically the people outside. But the sight of them strikes her dumb. She cowers
at the window.* GIDEON LEFROY *opens small door, L., and rushes over to the
table where his brother is standing.*)

GIDEON. Brother Morgan!

MORGAN. What are you here for, Gideon?

GIDEON. For judgment upon you because of your unrighteous
dealing.

MORGAN. You have been filling that dry skin of yours with your
righteous brandy.

GIDEON. I know that your iniquity is as a winter's night, dark
and terrible. Thou art hardened in thine iniquity. Thine iniquity is
as brass hardened in the workshop; yea, thou art all brass, and as
brass thou shalt be broken up, and not left standing any more. I have
been moved to say this to you.

MORGAN. Be off!

GIDEON. The mouth that has filled itself with curses shall be si-
lenced, Morgan.

MORGAN. What do you want? Tell me and get out of this.

GIDEON. Art thou sober, Morgan?

MORGAN. More sober than you are, you canting dog! (MORGAN
takes up the sword-stick as if to strike him with it.)

GIDEON. Yes, Morgan, you hold the rod of your iniquity before
me. This is it, this that you boast of for a sword-stick! Where did
it come from? You boast that you won it in your gambling riotings.
You staked a brace of bloodhounds against it. Now will your iniquity
be established. They were by a dog—

MORGAN. Out of this or I'll hurt you—I will, by God!

GIDEON. Hurt me as well as rob me, aye, you would do that,

Morgan. I ask you where the dog came from that that litter was by? He was here—I fed him here. I brought bones to that bloodhound, Morgan Lefroy. And who ever paid me for the nourishing of that dog? Not you, brother Morgan. (*Suddenly he puts his hands on the sword-stick and wrests it from* MORGAN, *and holds it in a way that shows he can be dangerous.*)

MORGAN. You'd be dangerous, would you? I'll show you that I can be dangerous too. (*He quickly draws a dagger from inside his coat.*)

GIDEON. Half, do you hear? I won't be cheated by you. I won't! I won't! I'll have it, I'll have it, I say. (*He goes to door to vestibule.* MOR-GAN *follows him. The door is slammed in* MORGAN'S *face. He returns to desk after slight pause at door. Holds dagger in his hand; pauses at desk; looks at dagger; takes it in left hand; leans hand holding dagger on desk; suddenly decides to follow* GIDEON, *and starts for door, leaving dagger on desk.* PEG THE BALLAD-SINGER *has been crouching by the window, not giving attention to the scene between the brothers.*)

PEG. Me to be condemned by the people, me that lay by their fires and ate the bit they gave me! Oh, the way they look at the house that I'm in! The way they look at it! (*She comes to* MORGAN LEFROY *as he is half-way to door. She is between him and the desk.*)

PEG. Oh, your honour, save me! Save me from those that have their eyes upon me.

MORGAN. Well, my good woman, I'll try to do that. I might have a regiment of soldiers brought to the town.

PEG. Oh, and would you let me be with the soldiers?

MORGAN. I might do that. And I could have you taken to the house of a magistrate where you would be safe.

PEG. Do that, your honour, and all my life I will pray for you.

MORGAN. Then you could be put on board of a ship and brought to another part of the country—to a part where the people would not know you.

PEG. Could I get to such a place?

MORGAN. You could. It will be done.

PEG. And my son? Oh, what will happen to Terence?

MORGAN. Your son too I'll look after. I will have him set at liberty. Indeed, he'll be in any part of the country that you want to stay in. I will get him a place in a gentleman's house, and you two can be together, safe and secure.

PEG. They told me you were hard and grinding to the people. Wasn't it well I didn't believe that! On my knees I thank you, and I pray for you.

MORGAN. Hush, my good woman; I'll do all I said for you.

PEG. The blessing of the poor and the shelterless be upon you. . . . But they . . . they'll think that I have betrayed the people.

MORGAN. It can't be helped. You'll have the name for that.

PEG. The name for that! That I betrayed the people! And I sat by their fires and lay in their houses!

MORGAN. It can't be helped, Peg. You'll have the name for having betrayed them, as they call it. Well, did you ever hear that it was as well to have the blame as the name?

PEG. What meaning is there in that?

MORGAN. This meaning, Peg. That as you have and will always have the name for having betrayed the people you might as well have the blame as well. Oh, yes, you might as well have the blame. Nothing will clear you in the minds of the people outside. Well, then, come on and tell me who it was killed Isaac Hackman?

PEG. I haven't said it! Not a word has passed my lips!

MORGAN. For them down there, every word has passed your lips. Come now and tell me. Who was it did it?

PEG. How could I tell you that? I never could name those names!

MORGAN. They believe you have told. They blame you for telling. Aye, and they will kill you for telling. A stone smashing your head, another stone breaking your neck, and then you'll be left lying in a ditch! Go out amongst them and that is what you will get. You'll be left lying there, and there will be no word more about you. You know that. Sentence has been passed on you for doing a thing. Now do it—do it to save yourself. Who was it killed Isaac Hackman?

PEG. I can't, I can't. No matter what befalls me I can't do that!

MORGAN. I have told you what I'll do for you. I'll summon a regiment of soldiers to the town. I'll have you taken to the house of a magistrate where you will be safe. Then you will be put on board of a ship and brought to a part of the country where no one will know anything about you, will not know what you have the name of being or the blame of doing. Are you listening to me? What else will you ask? I'll do everything else to save and shield you. All I want you to do is to give me the names that you are blamed already for giving me.

PEG. It was never in me to do that.

MORGAN. Then will you go amongst the people outside?

PEG. They would destroy me, they would destroy me! Save me, your honour, save me!

MORGAN. What will you do to save yourself?

PEG. Anything, your honour, anything!

MORGAN. Then give me the names of the people concerned in the murder of Isaac Hackman!

PEG (backing away from him). Their names will never cross these lips of mine.

MORGAN. Give me the names, or I'll have you thrown into the street amongst the people that will destroy you. (He crowds her until she is against desk. She stands with her back to it, her hands on the desk for support.)

PEG. No. Look at me as you like, but you will see that I am not going to do that. Ah, I was foolish to think that you had any wish for my son. For what wish could you have for the people? And what could be between you and them but hatred and broken trust? Why did I come here at all? Ah, you planned to bring me here so that the people might see me here with you and think that I had betrayed them! Ah, you planned it, and you planned it well, and you have taken me like the bird under the crib!

MORGAN. Yes, you are like the bird under the crib, and there's no way out for you. There's nothing that you can do now; there's nothing that you can do.

PEG. Nothing that I can do, nothing that I can do! (*Feeling for support on desk, her hands come into contact with dagger.*)

MORGAN. They're shouting something. What is it all about? (*He goes to window.* PEG *takes up dagger. She holds it as if it were something marvellous that had been put into her hands. She crosses to L.*)

PEG. What did you want of me?

MORGAN. The people who murdered Isaac Hackman will be taken soon. You and no one else will be blamed for their betrayal. Nothing will clear you. Well, take the only thing you can get — safety — and take it from me. Give me the names of the people who did the murder, and claim protection. Speak to me. Was it Mary Sullivan's son? Was it Honor Gowan's brother? (PEG *does not speak.*)

MORGAN. Something has come into the street. I can't understand what it is. You can hear them. Tell me what they are saying? (*He turns to window again.*)

PEG. Kill, kill, kill! That's what the people are saying. And can't you hear something from the blacksmith's forge? Strike! Strike! It tells that there are strokes prepared for the one who betrays the people. Strike! Strike! Strike! Oh, it can't be for me that the strokes are! (*She goes toward* MORGAN LEFROY, *whose back is turned. She goes slowly, holding dagger. As he is about to turn she stabs him in the neck.* MORGAN LEFROY *falls.*)

PEG. There he lies, the man who would have betrayed us all! Now I can walk amongst the people, for I have saved them. And if my son meets his death he can die without shame, for none of his race ever betrayed the people! (*The window is opened from the outside. The* BELLMAN *is seen holding himself against the window.*)

BELLMAN. The curse of the people on you and your race!

PEG. I have saved the people.

BELLMAN. The man under bonds has put others under bonds. To save his own breast from the bullet he made known the names of them that destroyed that tormentor — Isaac Hackman. Your son has betrayed the people!

PEG. O Mother of All Affliction!

CURTAIN

GLENDALOUGH

CHARACTERS

CHARLES STEWART PARNELL
ANNA, his sister
AN EMISSARY FROM THE PRIME MINISTER
THREE SANDWICH MEN
A FRIAR

CHORUSES

TWO HOODED MEN
THE BAND OF THE HAG OF GLENDALOUGH

APPARITIONS

KATHLEEN who is the Hag of Glendalough
GHOST of Henry Grattan
GHOST of Pigott
VOICES

SCENE: *In front of an ancient monastery. Two* MEN *stand outside; they wear cloaks with hoods that come over their foreheads so that little of their faces is seen.*

FIRST FIGURE. Saint Kevin was friendly to shepherds. He drove away the Morrigu, the Great Queen to whom they gave fleeces.

SECOND. They say she comes back to Glendalough.

FIRST. She comes back. She goes through all Ireland but she comes back.

SECOND. Here she is the Hag of Glendalough, no longer a queen.

FIRST. To some she is a young girl . . .

FIRST. Whom Kevin threw down the cliff and into a lake.

SECOND. Because she would not share his bed in the cave.

FIRST. The Morrigu, the stirrer-up of strife.

SECOND. The Hag of Glendalough.

FIRST. The young girl whom Kevin hurled into the lake.

SECOND. There are signs of her return. (*Their speech becomes a chant*)

FIRST. In lonely thoughtfulness
    There the heron stands,
    And there the crane's slow flight
    Is over darkened wave.

SECOND. These ever-lonely lakes!

FIRST. And should one who would know
    Life of his life come here,
    And walk along the edge
    Whereby the heron stands,
    And gaze upon the dark
    Wave, or lower down . . .

SECOND. Will hear the voices low
    His memory contains.

61

FIRST. Not all are fit to hear
        The voices by the lake.
SECOND. Only the one who can
        From vision pass to act
FIRST. The visionary man
        Who turns to give command

(*They go off. More of Glendalough is seen. A man stands by the lake deep in thought. He is recognizably* CHARLES STEWART PARNELL. *A woman who has evidently driven a vehicle — a whip is in her hand — comes to him. She is his sister* ANNA.)

PARNELL. Anna! Anna! What brings you here?

ANNA. I took the dog-cart and followed you from Avondale.

PARNELL. But why have you come in on my solitude, Anna? (*He says this good humouredly. As they talk they walk up and down.*)

ANNA. You were well guided, Charles.

PARNELL. Was I? Oh, in coming here, you mean.

ANNA. To a place where you can be alone, Charles.

PARNELL. Oh! And why have you come here to join me?

ANNA. Impulse. I saw you mount and ride from Avondale. I took out the dog-cart and followed you. This is the place to come to when you have so much, so much to consider.

PARNELL. The meeting in the Rotunda tomorrow night . . .

ANNA. Never in your life had you so much to consider.

PARNELL. That I know. A decisive meeting, Anna.

ANNA. The torches in the street outside, the thousands of faces, history being made.

PARNELL. Yes, yes, Anna. All that!

ANNA. And your triumph, Charles.

PARNELL. The gathering of the people of Ireland . . .

ANNA. Who will acclaim you as their leader!

PARNELL. Members of my party may leave me. The people of Ireland will not leave me — no, not even though their bishops condemn me.

ANNA (*solemnly*). They will not leave you.

PARNELL. All these thousands! They will never leave me. But why have you come into my solitude?

ANNA (*regarding him thoughtfully*). I will tell you when I get used to seeing you here.

PARNELL. And now that we're away from everything else, I'll show you something. (*He takes something treasured from his pocket. They stand together.*)

ANNA. A tress of hair!

PARNELL. Queenie's.

ANNA. Queenie! But Cathy was the name I heard from you.

PARNELL. For me a special name—Queenie. My wife's.

ANNA. The awful, awful ignominy of the divorce!

PARNELL. They tried to make it ignominious for me. The paid testimony of servant-girls to make me seem a lurking libertine! They knew—would dispute nothing. What did it matter if the divorce went through and Queenie was free to become my wife.

ANNA. Mrs Parnell!

PARNELL. The name is hers.

ANNA. It is still strange to me.

PARNELL. Ah, Anna, you cannot know what her love has meant to me! Every man—I'll say even the saints—has to have a woman in his life. There was none in mine till she came into it. She came into it nobly—like herself. Yes, there has to be a woman in a man's life. How could young men fight for a country so unfortunate as Ireland unless the country was shown to them as a woman?

ANNA. How many people believe that?

PARNELL. You will say members of my party deserted me because she was so much in my life that the bishops of Ireland have condemned me. And now that I've shown you what I would not show you in any other place, tell me why you have come here?

ANNA. I saw you this morning, Charles . . .

PARNELL. It doesn't seem as if you saw me domestically.

ANNA. You used to walk in your sleep.

PARNELL. I remember.

ANNA. When you came into the breakfast-room this morning, you were not walking in your sleep, of course—you looked so . . . I cannot think of a word, Charles . . . as if you were not with us. It was for that reason that I followed you.

PARNELL. Then I was in that state which I do not myself understand.

ANNA. And so I followed you here. Oh, not because I was alarmed at your state.

PARNELL. Haven't you all seen me like that before? And the reason you see me in my right self now is because I didn't come across a magpie on the road, and my horse didn't fall into a trot thirteen times. They call me superstitious. What does the word mean?

ANNA. My own belief is that what they call your superstition has some subtle connection with your geology, your trigonometry, your astronomy.

PARNELL. Superstitious! I am that, but what it means I don't know. Anyway, I'd never have burned the witches of old. Macbeth's mistake was not in consulting the witches, but only in believing the portion that pleased him in their advice.

ANNA. Now that I've seen you I'll wander about. You have to be alone.

PARNELL. Yes, the great assize!

ANNA. What is that?

PARNELL. It will be for me the great assize! And what have I to do before it? Give them words? Give them reasons? No. These are for meetings. Not Parliamentarianism there!

ANNA. Then what?

PARNELL. Myself. I give them myself.

ANNA. Yourself. Oh, yes, Charles. Yourself.

PARNELL. It comes readily to you, that word "yourself." A word too. As if it were a thing anyone could give on the moment of wanting to! Look at the heron flying across the dark lake.

ANNA. Yes, Charles.

PARNELL. He is searching for something not so hard to find as what I would give to the people of Ireland.

ANNA. And that is what you've come here to find! I know it.

PARNELL. And this is the place. Not Avondale. Not Dublin.

ANNA. By that lake whose gloomy shore
    Skylark never warbled o'er.

PARNELL. So that was Glendalough, was it? No skylarks here?

ANNA. We're told there aren't. In the song.

PARNELL. We used to hear Delia sing it. What was the reason for the skylarks forsaking Glendalough?

ANNA. Something St Kevin did —

    And with rude repulsive shock
    Hurled her from the beetling rock.

The rock is over there.

PARNELL. Who was hurled from it by the Saint?

ANNA. A girl who wanted to keep him company,

PARNELL. Wrong. Men don't hurl women from rocks for that.

ANNA. Saints act differently — that's why they're saints.

PARNELL. I reserve my opinion about that.

ANNA. A tragedy of love.

PARNELL. Tragedies of love are not so simple, Anna.

ANNA. I'll look at the rock from which Kathleen . . .

PARNELL. Kath . . .

ANNA. It is not so high after all. (*She goes*)

PARNELL. Anna, are you gone? What a change that cloud makes over Glendalough. (*The scene becomes dim;* PARNELL *is in the shadow. There is another figure now, also in the shadow. She is like the maiden in a nineteenth century engraving.*)

FIGURE. I am the one in the song — Kathleen.

    'Twas from Kathleen's eyes he flew,
    Eyes of most unholy blue.

Is the blue of my eyes unholy! Look into them, my king.

PARNELL. Only one has a right to name me so.

KATHLEEN. The one who has my name — Cathy. Well, if I can't say "my king" to you, I can say "Charles Stewart Parnell." It is a great day for me when the one with that name comes into my domain.

PARNELL. I have come to Glendalough to know the man that I am.

KATHLEEN. Oh, you'd give yourself — yourself — to the people. I've heard of them who would do that.

PARNELL. Not many could.

KATHLEEN. Oh, haughty Charles Stewart Parnell. What are you to them without the gains and the plans?

PARNELL. Their leader.

KATHLEEN. The world thinks that a leader ought to have plans and show gains.

PARNELL. I will not speak of gains and plans to the gathering to-morrow night.

KATHLEEN. But when you speak of who you are have memories of . . .

PARNELL (*to himself*). O'Shea. Queenie's anguished hour. The Party's reproaches . . .

KATHLEEN. And so you will not speak of gains and plans?

PARNELL. Gains! Plans! Where do they come in when I face the gathering of the people of Ireland?

KATHLEEN. Oh, haughty Charles Stewart Parnell! Oh, but won't you speak of other things?

PARNELL. What other things?

KATHLEEN (*in a more piercing voice*). Speak of them who are leaving you. Healy!

PARNELL. O'Brien!

KATHLEEN. Davitt!

PARNELL. Dillon!

KATHLEEN. Why are they leaving you?

PARNELL. The divorce that I was named in was not a moral issue.

Everyone who knew me knew that. The English tried to destroy me with forgeries. Then they had me named in the divorce in which I was not allowed to defend myself against the squalid charges.

KATHLEEN. And who would know that better than your party, Charles Stewart Parnell.

PARNELL. They do me a great wrong.

KATHLEEN (*vehemently*). Expose them for what they are to the gathering of the people of Ireland! Betrayers! Faction-makers! Make that gathering of the people of Ireland rise up and curse them! Curse them! Have them hounded through the length and breadth of Ireland! Davitt! Healy! O'Brien! Dillon! (PARNELL *raises his hand.*)

KATHLEEN. That is the way you will win the people of Ireland to you—they glory in seeing the betrayers scourged!

PARNELL. I did not come here to learn that.

KATHLEEN. Then the scourged will be you. The scourged will be you! By my old name of the Morrigu I swear that Ireland is going to see a scourging, a scourging, as great as ever she saw. (*She disappears.*) (*In the light that is still dim* PARNELL *stands in a trance-like position. A* VOICE *come to him.*)

VOICE. You have taken my wife and the mother of my children.

PARNELL. O'Shea. He speaks of years ago. She never was his. Ours is a steadfast love. I would give everything I have—everything I have, for the one he calls his wife.

VOICE. I have the right to the house. You can have her anywhere you want, but I'm in the bedroom.

PARNELL. This is to make a bargain with me.

VOICE. There was an old-fashioned way of settling this.

PARNELL. A duel in France.

VOICE. A way becoming to an army man as I am—Captain O'Shea. I am as good with the pistol as you are and I can have the first shot.

PARNELL. He is not thinking of a duel. He knows I would risk that.

VOICE. Parnell, we are men of the world. We don't want the world talking about our affairs. When the old woman dies and Kitty gets her fortune—she is the favorite niece, we all know—I'll let her get a divorce.

PARNELL. He will get a settlement—anything he asks for—when Kitty's aunt dies. To buy a man! And sell myself!

VOICE. The timber in the old dame is hard—we know that.

PARNELL. We know . . .

VOICE. Oh, No! You know nothing! You are busy with great affairs. Not to talk of making a cuckold of a man in Brighton! You can't be thinking of an old woman's last will and testament.

PARNELL. What demand will come from him?

VOICE. In the meantime a seat in Parliament would do something for me—under your leadership, Parnell.

PARNELL. It would be wrong for me to consider it. (*His voice becomes resolute*) Wrong for me to consider it, even.

VOICE. There is a vacant seat—Galway. It is at your disposal. O'Shea M.P. Member of the National Party.

PARNELL. The Chief of the Party could not . . . The Party must give me loyalty. I expect loyalty from the Party.

VOICE (*contemptuously*). Loyal! Loyal! Loyal Charles Stewart Parnell.

PARNELL. That is O'Shea! He would demean me!

VOICE. I know what you would say (*mockingly*): It is for the Party to consider. Don't prevaricate, Parnell!

PARNELL. He can say that to me!

VOICE. You are the master of the Party. No one within it can contradict you. Galway for O'Shea! O'Shea for Galway. Exchange Parnell! Galway for me! Brighton for you!

PARNELL. No! No! Never!

VOICE. It would be best for her, Parnell, to have me out of the way.

PARNELL. It means he would not molest her ever! Kitty free of him!

VOICE. I'd be away. London for me! I'd never go down to Brighton (*he hums it*), to Brighton, anymore.

PARNELL. Yes, I know what I am doing and why I am doing it!

VOICE. Give me Galway!

PARNELL. I will give him Galway! It will be plain to the Party why I give it! (*There is a cackle of laughter.* PARNELL, *his hands clenched, takes a step towards where it comes from. A* WOMAN'S VOICE *halts him.*)

VOICE. Charles! Charles!

PARNELL. This is sorrow for both of us! Sorrow that no one can ever know!

VOICE. Your arms, Charles, for the child.

PARNELL. Dead Queenie?

VOICE. And I could not have you near me. Yours and mine — our first child! (*As he stands with head bowed there are angry voices.*)

PARNELL. I am the only one who can accomplish what you want for Ireland. I can accomplish it for I am the only one who will not quail before your enemies. Pay me for this as you would pay one who serves you.

VOICE. By letting the people of Galway be served by a cur?

PARNELL. I make no excuses. (*The cloud has passed on. Parnell stands in a clear light. With his last words his appearance has become commanding. A* MAN *enters. His appearance marks him as an emissary from the British government.*)

EMISSARY. I took the liberty of borrowing a horse from your stable. I followed Miss Parnell and I have the advantage of finding you in this place.

PARNELL. You are from London?

EMISSARY. That is so. I think I am fortunate in finding you in this solitary place. What is this rather remarkable place, Mr Parnell?

PARNELL (*curtly*). Glendalough.

EMISSARY. An extremely appropriate place for a conference — if I may put myself in the position of having a conference with you, Mr Parnell. It is so difficult to find a place that is not public now that our newspaper reporters have become so enterprising.

PARNELL. Your people used to find a gaol convenient.

EMISSARY. A thing of the past, Mr Parnell—at least we hope it may become so.

PARNELL. From whom do you come?

EMISSARY. The Prime Minister. I can give you my credentials.

PARNELL. Your appearance is all you need give me.

EMMISSARY. I have the text of a proposal.

PARNELL. Signed.

EMISSARY. By the Prime Minister. I am an intermediary between you, Mr Parnell, and persons in the highest places.

PARNELL. I suppose your mission has to do with my speech to-morrow night.

EMISSARY. What the Prime Minister hopes to do, Mr Parnell, is to supply you with matter that would be helpful to you.

PARNELL. I speak to my fellow countrymen—not to a meeting of any crowd but my fellow countrymen who will be there from all quarters to hear me.

EMISSARY. That is understood, Mr Parnell.

PARNELL. Understood? By whom?

EMISSARY. By the person from whom I come.

PARNELL. Look around you, sir! Is there a place for parliamentarianism here?

EMISSARY. I have to deliver a message . . .

PARNELL. From an unrivalled sophist. Well, as soon as you are ready, sir.

EMISSARY. I might begin this way. The Prime Minister has many years of service before him. But taken by the calendar, he is an old man.

PARNELL. The last time I spoke to him I thought when he yawned he was about to die.

EMISSARY (*stiffly*). You have a dramatic way of putting it, Mr Parnell. We agree that the Prime Minister is an old man. He used a certain expression with regard to your leadership of the Irish Party.

PARNELL. He said that a great moral issue should have great

moral leadership and on that account I was not eligible for the leadership of a party that has Irish self-government for its goal. He told the Irish people that to obtain self-government they would have to jettison me.

EMISSARY. An old man! He spoke unguardedly.

PARNELL. Spoke! He wrote it. He would get rid of me. But he would have the Irish people do that for him.

EMISSARY. And your reply? Also written, Mr Parnell?

PARNELL. Do not throw me to the English wolves.

EMISSARY. A terrible expression to have used, if I may say so. Beyond . . .

PARNELL. Beyond parliamentarianism. But your message, sir?

EMISSARY (*playing for an interval*). I should say that this is a place I would have chosen for my communication.

PARNELL. It was designed for something else, I assure you.

EMISSARY. No doubt. Historic, of course. Mr Parnell, I am authorized to tell you that the sentence went far beyond what was in the Prime Minister's mind. His secretary caught at a passing phrase and wrote it into the letter. I have a letter in my pocket which can be published in to-morrow's Dublin journals saying this. His secretary will resign.

PARNELL. I like the secretary. I am sorry he has to take the blame for an old man's unguarded expression. But in a while he can be restored. Is not that so?

EMISSARY. I am an intermediary between the Prime Minister and yourself. What I have to say in that capacity affects your country and yourself.

PARNELL. Yes. And now we can get on.

EMISSARY. In your address to your countrymen (and the Prime Minister realizes it will be of the greatest significance to you and the people of Ireland), you will be able to give them a hopeful—indeed the triumphal news—that the Prime Minister will work with you.

PARNELL. You say it will be in the journals?

EMISSARY. I will take it to the editors to-day.

PARNELL. Well, that will be enough.

EMISSARY. What do you mean, Mr Parnell?

PARNELL. The people will have read it.

EMISSARY (*incredulous*). You mean that you will not use it as material for your speech? (PARNELL *shrugs and turns away. The* EMISSARY *is nonplussed. He makes a new approach.*)

EMISSARY. I am instructed to say that the Prime Minister will press on with the Home Rule Bill.

PARNELL (*interested*). Yes?

EMISSARY. Yes. He will even agree to include matters that you pressed him about.

EMISSARY. The Constabulary to come under an Irish government . . . Revenue . . .

PARNELL (*to himself*). Important! It may be worth all I have been through!

EMISSARY. Remember, Mr Parnell, that the phrase you used about English wolves has caused much resentment in England.

PARNELL. It was addressed to my countrymen.

EMISSARY. Quite so. But it rankles even amongst sections that support you. For that reason the Prime Minister suggests that Mr Justin MacCarthy be conspicuously associated with the Irish interest in the House.

PARNELL. Justin MacCarthy!

EMISSARY. The country recognizes him as an Irishman who has no enmity to England.

PARNELL. Where would I be?

EMISSARY. You would be present.

PARNELL. And speak?

EMISSARY. I suppose on matters that would not involve controversy.

PARNELL. There would be two Irish Parties in the House? One under my leadership and one under Justin MacCarthy's?

EMISSARY. The larger party adhering to you—as you have it already. Those who stay with you, and those who do not accept your leadership.

PARNELL. I reject the Prime Minister's proposal.

EMISSARY (*perplexed*). But I have made it perfectly understandable to you?

PARNELL. Perfectly.

EMISSARY (*still perplexed*). And the Prime Minister's letter withdrawing his objection to your leadership?

PARNELL. It need not be published.

EMISSARY. Mr Parnell, do you not think you owe an explanation to the Prime Minister?

PARNELL. Not to him. To you. I should not make it a mere dismissal.

EMISSARY (*stiffly*). My mission is finished.

PARNELL. But not my civility. Look! (*Almost involuntarily he points out the scene.*) We do not want to be subject to your country. Powerful people in your country want to hold us subject. To throw off subjection we must have power. We cannot raise a fighting force. Even if we could there is no place to retreat to after a check. We are not America. A six weeks' campaign would end whatever effort we could make. But there is one source of power your politicians overlooked when they took our parliament from us.

EMISSARY. I am sensible of your goodness . . .

PARNELL. They left us with eighty members in your House of Commons. That number is our source of power. Unified, drilled, obeying a single leader, they can be used to control your parties. We can force governments out and keep governments in.

EMISSARY. You have made us understand that already.

PARNELL. There must be for us a single party, a single command. Otherwise our members would be absorbed into one or another of your parties. Eighty men under my command is the only power Ireland possesses. To agree to the Prime Minister's proposal would be to throw away the power that has become formidable through me. Have you heard the name of Henry Grattan?

EMISSARY. Yes. A great orator.

PARNELL. He had the name of being a statesman. He did what no statesman should do. He let the armed force that brought him into power be disbanded. (GHOST *of Henry Grattan appears. At first he has the noble appearance shown in his statue. After a proud delivery he becomes decrepit.*)

GRATTAN. I found Ireland on her knees, I watched over her with paternal solicitude; I have traced her progress from injuries to arms, and from arms to liberty. Ireland is now a nation. In that character hail her, and bowing to her august presence, I say *ESTO PERPETUA.* (*Then, with bowed figure and in a feeble voice*) The Parliament of Ireland did risk everything, and are now nothing; and in their extinction left this instruction, not to their posterity, for they have none, but to you who come in the place of their posterity, not to depend on a sect of religion, not trust the final issue of your fortunes to anything less than the whole of your people. The Parliament of Ireland — of that assembly I have a paternal recollection. I sat by her cradle, I am following her hearse. (*He disappears.*)

PARNELL. The proposal would make ineffectual the only power we Irish have.

EMISSARY. May I say something in a friendly spirit, Mr Parnell.

PARNELL. Say it.

EMISSARY. The Prime Minister is an old man. Should he not succeed in putting through the Home Rule measure — and you are making that difficult for him — he will retire. Are any of his possible successors favorable to Irish self-government? Sir William Harcourt?

PARNELL. An able man, but self-government for Ireland means nothing to him.

EMISSARY. Lord Roseberry?

PARNELL. An unaccountable man. Ireland means nothing to him. But they will do what we force them to do.

EMISSARY. How long might it be until you have an opportunity to use your force?

PARNELL. Five years.

EMISSARY. In the meantime, Mr Parnell, there will be defections from your party. Mr MacCarthy you have lost. Also Mr O'Brien, Mr Davitt, Mr Healy. Others will go with them.

PARNELL. To-morrow night the people of Ireland will give me ample power.

EMISSARY. May I say that you are too proud to be the leader of a party?

PARNELL. I am the leader of a nation.

EMISSARY. I have no more to say, Mr Parnell. I will have to report to the Prime Minister—with great regret—that my mission has failed.

PARNELL. You will go back to Avondale. I hope you will allow my house to offer you hospitality before you leave.

EMISSARY. I have already had the offer. Yes, and I will be taken to my train. I will restore the horse to your stable.

PARNELL. Oh, yes, the horse.

EMISSARY (*as firing a parting shot*). Not the horse named . . . Dictator. (*He goes.*)

PARNELL. A Dictator! It is that they use against me. (*Smiling*) It is on their files somewhere. (*He goes off. The cloud resting above makes obscurity again. There is a clashing sound. A* BAND *of ragged, evil-looking people, men and women, appear. Conspicuous among them for a certain haughtiness of bearing is the* HAG OF GLENDALOUGH.)

BAND (*They dance as they sing*).

There was a time a likely lad with load would bring him gain,
His chieftain's head beneath his cloak, would pass through
    our domain,
And we would show him all our sports, the right old sports,
    bedad,

And grease his cabbage with pig's face, that likely, stirring lad!
        The sports we have, the right old sports, we'd show
            him these bedad!

To Dublin Castle where a hand is full as it is free
With silver for a chieftain's head he'd course it luckily,
And we would cheer his way because of nature true
To her, the Hag of Glendalough, our queenly Morrigu.
        To her, the Hag of Glendalough,
            We'll have all Ireland true.

A CRONE. They asked me who you were.
LEADER (*contemptuously*). Who asked you that, Big Mouth?
CRONE. The conjurors who make camp
        Beside the stunted tower.
LEADER. Tell her who I am.
THIRD CRONE. She is the one who owned
            The Glen of the Two Lakes
            Before this Kevin came
            He brought the men who prayed
            For the men who rule the tribes,
            And for the men who stand
            In Council Hall, and win
            Men to a firmer course.
LEADER. I spit on such a rule.
ANOTHER CRONE. But still he did not drive
            The Morrigu away
            From this, her old domain
            The Glen of the Two Lakes.
CRONE. This is her own domain,
        The Glen of the Two Lakes.
CHORUS. It is! It is! It is!
CRONE. She will forsake us! Something tells me she is on the move!

ANOTHER. Oh, she knows when she has to go somewhere else —
I can tell you that. She'll go into the towns — the little towns and the
big towns. And, believe me, the Hag of Glendalough will stir them
up, wherever she goes.

HAG (*suddenly turning on them*). I belong to all Ireland, I do. The
North and the South, the East and the West. I go to give myself to
all Ireland.

BAND. To all Ireland! For all Ireland! The Morrigu is for all
Ireland! (*They go off. Brightness comes again.* THREE MEN *carrying billboards
come on. They seat themselves on a low wall. The boards have newspaper announcements front and back: "Parnell Condemned by Bishops."*)

FIRST MAN. I got pushed into a ditch by a fellow who said he was
sorry I wasn't a bishop.

SECOND. It wasn't me or I'd have given him a crack on the skull
for saying a word against a bishop.

THIRD (*gravely*). I've a brother who is an evicted tenant.

SECOND. They'd all be restored to their holdings if your Parnell
hadn't been thinking about his woman.

FIRST MAN. I wish to God I had a woman to be thinking about.
I do be thinking about one, anyway, walking the roads with the boards
back and front of me. (PARNELL *comes on,* ANNA *with him.*)

PARNELL. An emissary, Anna! Credentials to show!

ANNA (*excited*). They have had to come to you, Charles!

PARNELL. From the Prime Minister.

ANNA. I knew — and didn't you know, too, Charles — that something would befall you in Glendalough!

PARNELL. The Prime Minister would withdraw his opposition to
me as a leader of the party.

ANNA (*with delight*). Charles! That means you are at the end of
the battle! What a statement to make to the meeting to-morrow night!
Oh, I knew you'd win!

PARNELL. Not that way. I rejected the Prime Minister's offer.

ANNA (*at a loss*). I suppose you had your reason to.

PARNELL. Trust me, Anna, as I want the people of Ireland to trust me. (PARNELL *sees the billboards with the announcements.*)

PARNELL (*reading*). The Bishops of Ireland condemn Parnell.

ANNA. Our enemies have taken over that newspaper.

PARNELL. The country knows their Lordships have condemned me. Why has it to be posted on the roads? (*To one of the* MEN) Where did you come from?

FIRST MAN. From Rathdrum, sir.

SECOND MAN. Every yard of the way from Rathdrum.

THIRD MAN. Mr Parnell, I know you, sir. Would you mind what a simple man would say to you, sir? (PARNELL *makes a sign of assent.*) It's about the families that were put out of their houses and their lands. They are walking the streets of towns with their hopes in you, Mr Parnell—that you'd get them back to their farms.

PARNELL. The evicted tenants? Did I not say "Keep a firm grip on your homesteads"? The men who kept that grip and the men who were unable to keep that grip, they are my men, and I am pledged to support them.

THIRD MAN. Well do we know it, Mr Parnell.

SECOND MAN. The bishops know something too, I'm telling you. (*A* FRIAR *comes on. He has something of a foreign appearance. He and* ANNA PARNELL *recognize each other. He is about to turn back when* ANNA *speaks to him.*)

ANNA. Father Mathurin!

(*The* FRIAR *raises his hand to prevent her drawing* PARNELL's *attention to him.* PARNELL *notices him.*)

FRIAR. Miss Parnell, would you make me known to your brother?

ANNA. This, Charles, is Father Mathurin, who has been helpful to us in the Land League.

PARNELL. Can you order these men to go away?

FRIAR. Perhaps, Mr Parnell, you lay too much stress on "order." I will request them to go away. (*He speaks to the* MEN. *They rise and shuffle off.*)

PARNELL. Your bishops should tell the people why they waited three weeks before denouncing me. If what I did is immoral, it was immoral three weeks ago. Do they think I am more helpless now than I was three weeks ago? Or do they think they will have to strip off some of my armour before I face the people of Ireland?

FRIAR. I cannot answer these questions. Miss Parnell knows that my good will is towards you.

ANNA. Father Mathurin is not long over from France.

FRIAR. From France, whose state shows what the state of Ireland may come to.

PARNELL. In what way, pray?

FRIAR. People against priests, the Church against the community, clericalism and anti-clericalism.

PARNELL. Have your bishops foreseen that? Or are you here to warn me?

FRIAR. I cannot continue the discussion, since I can give you no evidence of my good faith. I have stated—I am in a better position to state this than any parish priest or curate in Ireland—that, as you are not of our faith, the bishops have no right to judge you by a law that you have not been brought up in.

PARNELL. I have judged myself. After that the people of Ireland will judge me.

FRIAR. I am thinking of happenings that can grow worse and worse, more and more disastrous for the country—priests filled with their own importance, blackthorn sticks in their hands, leading bemused men against your and your followers' platforms, of irrevocable words said from the pulpit or the altar, of priests turned away from God, of husbands and wives, brothers and sisters making homes places of strife. I have seen how such things divide and dishonor a country.

PARNELL. Will your bishops be persuaded to withdraw what they have said about me?

FRIAR. If you hold your party together, if the people are solidly behind your party, the bishops would be like so many Achilleses in their tents, I should think.

PARNELL. We would be spared the contentions you have witnessed in France. But you see another way.

FRIAR. I, Mr Parnell?

PARNELL. Maybe you. Certainly others.

FRIAR. I am here by chance, believe me.

PARNELL. I will do you the justice to believe that. But you know that there are those who are convinced that if I resigned my leadership temporarily . . .

ANNA. Not one woman in our league wants that.

PARNELL. If my place were taken by some member of the party, then, when the storm was over, I could resume my leadership with a peaceable Ireland behind me.

FRIAR. You speak as if you had considered this.

PARNELL. I have. A battle is opening and I have to consider this and that tactic.

FRIAR. A battle *is* opening. What is it for?

PARNELL. To save the country from a situation that it was left in before.

FRIAR. And what is that, sir?

PARNELL. The situation that Henry Grattan left it in.

FRIAR (*perplexed*). Grattan?

ANNA. Our grandfather was with Grattan. The picture in Avondale shows the two of them together.

PARNELL. Grattan gave up the only power Ireland could use. The result was disunion and subjection. His power was in armed men. Mine is in a disciplined party. If that Party can remain united and disciplined under a leader other than myself . . .

FRIAR (*with much sympathy*). You would resign your leadership temporarily?

PARNELL. It is a question of tactics. The meeting to-morrow night may show me what to do.

FRIAR. Entering a battle! I who come from France know the way such a battle could be pitched! (*He bows his head as if saying a prayer.*)

ANNA. He has only to stand before them! They will be trees shaken to their roots!

FRIAR (*speaking as if to himself*). I was there when he turned on his accusers in the House of Commons. Not as a man brought to judgment, but as a man bringing judgment. When he spoke I knew the old Ireland was gone. It will be like that every time he speaks for himself. Thousands will not know it. But men who are now in their boyhood will know. They will change Ireland because an image will reach them of the man standing there. (*Taking leave, he addresses* PARNELL.) I am happy to have come on you in such a sacred place. I am here as a pilgrim. (*To* ANNA) I am visiting the churches. Seven, I am told.

ANNA. Much less than that number, you'll find.

FRIAR (*bowing to* ANNA *as he goes*). Miss Parnell, your brother has my good wishes, even my prayers. (*He goes.*)

ANNA. He has left us without doing anything for us.

PARNELL. What should he have done for us?

ANNA (*humorously*). Shown Charles Stewart Parnell who Charles Stewart Parnell is.

PARNELL. Glendalough—no less than Glendalough—can show me that.

ANNA (*banteringly*). Charles Stewart Parnell he is
Who's here to test the gold
Washings that are in Wicklow streams
As in the days of old.

PARNELL (*smiling*). No, Anna. The metallurgist Parnell is not here.

ANNA. Charles Stewart Parnell he is
The lord of instruments,
Who asteroids and comets knows
Through his own measurements.

PARNELL. No, Anna. The astronomer Parnell is not here. Look! The ground has been turned up there. Buried things are out of the clay. (ANNA *takes up an object.*)

ANNA. What is it?

PARNELL (*examining it*). A sword-hilt, no less.

ANNA. From the old times?

PARNELL. This place for all its piety was attacked often. Look at the tower over there? It was a stronghold. They saved their treasures there.

ANNA (*picking up another object*). What is this?

PARNELL (*becoming excited*). A pike-head! This is a real find, Anna! The Wicklow and Wexford men held out here with their pikes. Michael Dwyer may have been here. In Aughnavanagh, outside the shooting-lodge . . .

ANNA. Go on, Charles.

PARNELL. They were there. The stone is beside the door — the stone they sharpened their pike-heads on. These grey-coated men with their pikes. Would that I had them with me today! They gave all they had for Ireland.

ANNA. You have the same men. They will be at the gathering to-morrow night.

PARNELL (*after a moment's reflection*). How extraordinary, Anna!

ANNA. What is extraordinary?

PARNELL. That I came to Glendalough and found this! Aughnavanaugh and my thoughts on the hillside beside the stone! I love the men that I saw before me then! I love the people of Ireland.

ANNA. And you are the man who is to address them to-morrow night. Charles Stewart Parnell!

PARNELL. Yes. I know myself now. And there are other things in Glendalough that have brought me to know myself. (*He speaks in a low voice to himself.*) The one who called herself Kathleen! The voices! (*He speaks to* ANNA.) That emissary, Anna! Your priest! The man who spoke of the evicted tenants.

ANNA. They made you know yourself! Charles Stewart Parnell! You will have him speak and all Ireland will respond.

PARNELL. Be contented, Anna!

ANNA. The women will be there, Charles. My Ladies' Land League foremost. Now I'll go and find Father Mathurin and drive him to Dundrum.

PARNELL. Oh, Anna! Anna! (*He smiles.*) Parliamentarianism in Glendalough!

ANNA. What do you mean, Charles?

PARNELL. You will indoctrinate the good priest as you drive him to Dundrum.

ANNA. For the Ladies' Land League, Charles. (*She goes. The place dims as* PARNELL *stands there, his arms folded. The* GHOST OF PIGOTT *the Forger appears.*)

PIGOTT. I am here, close to you, Parnell.

PARNELL. Pigott the Forger!

PIGOTT. I was always a good hand with the pen. (*Mournfully*) How would I know my spelling would be the ruin of me?

PARNELL. Your mind was the ruin of you.

PIGOTT. Aye, Parnell, the mind! That's where all the forgeries come from.

PARNELL. You would have ruined me, ruined the cause, for a price.

PIGOTT. The price isn't always in cash. It was for me, of course. You lived in a grand house, Parnell. You never knew the need of money, with your horses and your servants, your grouse-shooting and your rent-roll. I worked for cheap newspapers and bought pictures of naked women with what was left over when I paid for my lodging.

PARNELL. You were yourself when you were a forger—yourself.

PIGOTT. You don't know the whole story, Parnell.

PARNELL. A tedious story!

PIGOTT. Oh, no. I made myself a leader. I was the leader of those who plotted against you, Parnell. There is always the secret, the unmentioned plot against the leader. I was the one who forwarded the unmentioned plot. Oh, I got the money for what I did. I sold the letters that made you a criminal in the eyes of those who read

the great English newspaper—"Parnellism and Crime" was the title.
I was good with the pen. It's a talent, you know.

PARNELL. You got your fee.

PIGOTT. I wanted to get into history.

PARNELL (*amazed*) You! How?

PIGOTT. I am in history. Pigott, Parnell, Pigott! (*With a passion
of longing*) You think that where you go to-morrow night you will be
received as a king—torches blazing in the streets outside, thousands
of faces looking up at you . . .

PARNELL. The faces . . .

PIGOTT. The bands, the cheers.

PARNELL. The people of Ireland.

PIGOTT. Again I will be close to you.

PARNELL. No. No.

PIGOTT. Don't you know the forger is always close to the leader?
The forger is part of the leader. You knew that when you were with
the Grand Old Man. There's a forger there. The man's forgery of
his principles. And that's what you'll give them, Parnell, to-morrow
night, a forgery of the man who fought for the tenants, who made
the English offer self-government to Ireland.

PARNELL. What right have you to remind me of your existence?
You were covered with ignominy! You shot yourself!

PIGOTT. It will always be with me, the scene in the House of Commons when I stood before the counsel, the eyes of all on me, some
praying that I would get the better of him and that, there and then,
they would see the dominating Irishman ruined, and some sure they
would see the counsel get the better of me and give you the greatest
triumph a man ever had in that place! That is the scene that I go
through, that goes through me.

PARNELL. A lie was stamped into the ground before my enemies
and my friends and in the face of all the world.

PIGOTT. Why did I let it be done before your enemies and your
friends and in the face of the world? I had confessed to the forgeries.

All I had to do was sign the confession and get away with my price — my good price. But that wouldn't do for Pigott. Not at all! As I walked down the London street I made up my mind. I would make a stand before the world.

PARNELL. It is nothing to me. You faltered. You broke down. You shot yourself in a hotel room. What is it to me? What is it to the world?

PIGOTT. My last copy of Parnell.

PARNELL. Back to hell with you!

PARNELL. This is no time for the dead and gone! Pigott and his forgeries! But if I can believe I heard from a ghost there was a truth in what he said! The leader has a forger beside him! Did he say inside him! He forges a person out of himself! That unrivaled sophist has done that! No one will ever say that Charles Stewart Parnell has done that! (*He moves forward as if to address a crowd. His figure becomes more erect and his voice takes on more intensity.*) You have heard me so far. I do not pretend that I had not moments of trial and temptation, but I do claim that never in thought, word, or deed that I have been false to the trust that the Irish people have confided in me. (*As he stands with hand outstretched the song of the Morrigu and her band is heard.*)

PIGOTT. Oh, don't be so violent. I wanted to have the drama, as you want to appear King of Ireland to-morrow night. But remember the forger, Parnell — the forger close to you, the forger in yourself. (*He disappears.*)

PARNELL (*alone but commanding*). No words, no look that my life is not behind! That will be my answer to the sophists and the condemners. The people of Ireland will know me then and will know my love for them. On their love I will stand whether my life is for months or years. I may change Ireland by laws — it was that I wanted to do. I will change Ireland by the resolve that has come to me here.

CURTAIN

MONASTERBOICE

CHARACTERS

JAMES JOYCE
EMMA CLEARY
JOHN STANISLAUS JOYCE
MR. MACANASPEY

CHORUSES

TWO FIGURES, HOODED MEN
TWO GUARDIANS

APPARITIONS

KATHLEEN who is the Hag of Glendalough
VOICES

The entrance to an ancient monastic establishment. TWO FIGURES *wearing hoods suggestive of monastic times appear.*

> FIRST FIGURE. Although no marauders
> Have burst into it for a thousand years
> This place we guard.
> SECOND FIGURE. The thrush nests in the yew
> Within the reach of hand, but none
> Disturbs her on the nest.
> FIRST FIGURE. For this is Monasterboice, a place forsaken,
> But not abandoned — no.

(A blare is heard from a CROWD *at some distance.)*

> SECOND FIGURE. How troubling is the noise!
> FIRST FIGURE. 'Twill last a summer's day!
> SECOND FIGURE. And what we guard
> The Cross of Muiredach, is here to show
> Man's fall, his new ascent, and then
> His progress, troubled or laughable,
> All on the granite that the earth reserves
> For long-enduring works.
> FIRST FIGURE. And then the circle
> Around the cross that tells us the beginning
> Is in the end, the end in the beginning.
> As long as we keep faith
> No feuds can shatter it.
> SECOND FIGURE. Although the army that would make
> Scots Bruce the King of Ireland lost their cause
> In field nearby, no soldiers swarmed in
> To push war's furrow through the sacred place.

FIRST FIGURE. Even those spiteful men,
The pack of Cromwell, with gaze on images,
Did not bay round the Cross of Muiredach.

(*The* HAG OF GLENDALOUGH *comes on. The* GUARDIANS *raise hands to hold her off.*)

HAG. Sometime your place for me, but that's not yet:
I go where music blares and the loud shout is heard:
They'll break your Cross to spite one another soon.
FIRST GUARDIAN. Pass on!
HAG. I am the Great Queen. I am Morrigu.
SECOND GUARDIAN. You have not entered here. You cannot enter.
HAG. You'll hear the ballad I delight to sing. (*She sings screechingly.*)

From Gibbet Glade through Gibbet shade a likely lad
    would go,
His Chieftain's head beneath his cloak in Castle Yard to
    show.
The better off that lad will be when he can turn and say
    The Chief out of my way.

And we will cheer that likely lad — hurrow, hurrow,
    hurrow!
For to the Hag of Glendalough he gives allegiance due.
And may he always get full price who brings a Chieftain
    down,
And raise the head, the eyeless head, for eyes of all the
    town.
The Queen, the Great Queen, I'm the one who'll make of
    him my own!

(*She goes. The* GUARDIANS *move to the pillar that is the sun-dial*)

FIRST GUARDIAN. This is the place
Where Time is measured by the sacred hours.

SECOND GUARDIAN (*ringing a little bell*). Prime, Sext, Compline . . .

FIRST GUARDIAN. Good Friday's hymn we'll chant. (*They chant a hymn in Latin. As they go off, a* YOUNG MAN *and a* GIRL *come on. They are* JAMES JOYCE *and* EMMA CLEARY.)

EMMA. Do you often repeat it?

JOYCE. The Latin hymn? Oh, yes. (*Indicating where the* CROWD *is*) An antidote to our Irish oratory.

EMMA. So you bring me under the influence of St. Thomas Aquinas! Isn't it his hymn? (*She says this with a laugh that is somewhat affected.*)

JOYCE. And properly—since the monastic smell still lingers here.

EMMA. I prefer to hear what you were saying, you know.

JOYCE. We met at the outskirts of the crowd after a long interval of not seeing each other, and you brought me here. Why?

EMMA. Because we were near Monasterboice.

JOYCE. Well?

EMMA. It was as if my guardian angel told me—this is the place for James Joyce. Ireland is here. (*She points to the great cross.*)

JOYCE (*seeing something on top of the cross and not knowing what it is*). What is resting on it?

EMMA (*With some amazement*). A hawk, I do believe.

JOYCE (*excitedly*). Do you know it is a hawk?

EMMA. It is. *An Seabhac* in Irish.

JOYCE. The hawk-headed man! The man with wings! Daedalus!

EMMA. Who?

JOYCE. The one I've borrowed an identity from.

EMMA. Oh, have you?

JOYCE. Stephen Daedalus! Myself!

EMMA. Baptized by yourself?

JOYCE. Isn't there baptism of water, of blood, of desire?

EMMA. The catechism says so. But when you were taking a name—I suppose it was to write your poetry under—why didn't you take an Irish one?

JOYCE (*Intoning the name druidically*). Mananaun MacLir!

EMMA. Your hawk has flown to the tower. (*Good humoredly*) That's where your mockery gets you. (*He turns to the tower at the back. Then He stands with averted head, the buoyancy gone from him.*)

EMMA (*enthusiastically*). Here is where we begin after a thousand years.

JOYCE (*wearily*). Back of this! Over here!

EMMA. Burial! New graves in Monasterboice! (*The sound of spades is heard.*)

JOYCE. The hawk! The spade! Where have I come to?

EMMA. Why do you, James Joyce, say we begin there? I spoke of the Cross of Monasterboice.

JOYCE. We begin with an act.

EMMA. But burial . . . ?

JOYCE. An act that is irrevocable! With that we begin.

EMMA (*abashed by something significant in his look*). What act of yours have you to think of here?

JOYCE. Refusal.

EMMA. A prayer is being said out there.

JOYCE. Unasked for! That is a mercy! (*To the sound of the ringing of spades at the back the words of litany are heard.*)

> Mother most amiable,
> Mother most admirable,
> Mother of good counsel.

(*There are murmurs and a final ring of the spade. Then silence at the back.*)

EMMA. I believe I know. Your mother died without your giving her the consolation of joining with her in a prayer.

JOYCE. Words I could not believe in.

EMMA. It was wrong, no matter what you believe.

JOYCE. *Non serviam.*

EMMA. Whose are the words?

JOYCE. Lucifer's.

EMMA. Perhaps we should not have come here. I still could make myself useful at the meeting.

JOYCE. Do you know the litany of that noble young Jesuit, Saint Aloysius?

EMMA. I have had no occasion to know it.

JOYCE. I'll recite the part that applies particularly to me—

> Most chaste youth,
> Angelic youth,
> Most humble youth,
> Model of young students,
> Despiser of riches,
> Enemy of vanities,
> Scorner of honors,
> Mirror of mortification,
> Mirror of perfect obedience,
> Lover of evangelical poverty.

EMMA. I could pray for you.

JOYCE. You were not thinking of that when you brought me here.

EMMA (*an explanation forced from her*). Our country is having a renaissance and you should be in our ranks.

JOYCE (*looking at her significantly*). For what reward?

EMMA (*primly*). That's a matter I don't go into. Well, there is the Cross of Muiredach, our last native creation.

JOYCE. I observe it as something well done.

EMMA (*passing from some embarrassment*). The great circle! It must mean something to your philosophical mind.

JOYCE. Or to my writer's mind.

EMMA (*becoming more assured*). And then the figures covering back and front and sides. There is a history of the human race! When will we have an artist who will have such a conception?

JOYCE. At present I am interested in presenting one person.

EMMA. Who is that?

JOYCE. Stephen Daedalus.

EMMA (*somewhat deflated*). And now you know why I brought you here.

JOYCE. To take me from parliamentarianism to the new nationalism.

EMMA. Well, shouldn't you be with the younger people who know that the fight is not for institutions but for the soul of a country?

JOYCE. What is the name of the Irish god of love?

EMMA. Angus.

JOYCE. I'd like to believe that it was Angus brought us to this secluded place.

EMMA. Out there they are speaking of your hero, Parnell.

JOYCE. Who else have they to speak of?

EMMA. Well, Stephen Daedalus, Parnell is dead.

JOYCE (*with bitter anger*). Because of the action of the bold and chivalrous Irish people whose soul you would save. And Mr. O'Brien is still denouncing Mr. Healy, and Mr. Healy is employing the barbed arrows of his wit.

EMMA. Do you admire his wit?

JOYCE. When Parnell told them "I am the master of the party," Healy had the wit to say, "And who is the mistress?" Brilliant! To answer a declaration of leadership with another quip! Listen to the cheers as one faction rises to triumph over the other!

EMMA. And what brought you there, Stephen Daedalus?

JOYCE. You did.

EMMA. Shall I say perhaps I did.

JOYCE. Another perhaps.

EMMA. Go on.

JOYCE. On the library steps last night I overheard you say that you were going to the meeting to distribute your Gaelic League leaflets. You did not let me see you for a long time. The last night I walked with you . . .

EMMA. Along Stephen's Green.

JOYCE. I had been gazing out of a window in the College when I saw you pass. I saw a young woman walking proudly through a decayed city. You were proud of being young and proud of being a woman. I saw it in the way you walked.

EMMA. And you the young man that everybody talked about.

JOYCE. I was full of despair. I live a strange life without help or sympathy from anyone. When I was cursing my days I saw you. There is a human creature at last, I said. I had to jump up and rush out.

EMMA. And then you said to me as we stood before our house . . .

JOYCE. I said to you I will be in the garden. Open your window and call my name. Ask me to come to you. Then open your door and let me come in.

EMMA. Then we didn't see each other for a long time. And when we were on the steps of the library . . .

JOYCE. And I overheard . . .

EMMA. I intended you should overhear.

JOYCE. I was right in saying you were a human being. You have brought me to this secluded place. Why?

EMMA. You are a poet, and I want you to say one of your poems to me.

JOYCE. You are a young woman. I am a young man.

EMMA. Say one of your poems.

JOYCE.

> Bid adieu, adieu, adieu,
> Bid adieu to girlish days,
> Happy love is come to woo
> Thee and woo thy girlish ways—
> The zone that doth become thee fair,
> The snood upon thy yellow hair.
>
> When thou hast heard his name upon
> The bugles of the cherubim
> Begin thou softly to unzone

> Thy girlish bosom unto him
> And aftly to undo the snood
> That is the sign of maidenhood.

EMMA. You say nothing about love — I mean your own love. You said nothing about love outside the house that evening.

JOYCE. Youth and desire. They are real.

EMMA. I felt that.

JOYCE. Why were you not human being enough to come to the window?

EMMA. The room was mine. My own.

JOYCE. What should I offer to give for what is your own — your maidenhood?

EMMA. What you have never said — love.

JOYCE. One gives freely.

EMMA. Tell me what?

JOYCE. Their bodies when they love.

EMMA. That is gross. But you can say such things. It is as if you were brought up under a different dispensation from the rest of us.

JOYCE. I was brought up under the same dispensation. But I've looked outside it.

EMMA. I could never look outside.

JOYCE. Oh, yes, you can. The softness that came into your eyes that evening showed me that.

EMMA. You are imaginative. Tell me another poem of yours.

JOYCE. Let us keep to the non-imaginative. From the library steps where we stood last night you have brought me here.

EMMA. Only that I might see you again. Only that we might be friends. Only that you might become an Irishman of the new movement. Now I know you better.

JOYCE. What do you know about me?

EMMA. You do not speak of love.

JOYCE. I say that I am a man. I say that you are a woman.

EMMA. What man would ask a girl—a girl he respected—and not protect her from the consequence?

JOYCE. What consequence?

EMMA. The loss of her good name for one.

JOYCE. More of our servility.

EMMA (*sharply*). Is that your answer?

JOYCE. The servility that I see in the streets, in the college, that I hear in the cheering out there. Yes, the servility that Parnell was above, that has made his memory sacred to me.

EMMA. There is no servility in your dispensation. Nor love, either.

JOYCE. One gives freely. There is no servility then.

EMMA. And marriage?

JOYCE. I do not understand the word.

EMMA. Word! Is that what it is for you?

JOYCE. You are asking: would I make myself one of the servile crowd to have the right to you? Father Butt could find me a clerk-ship in the Brewery. We would have a house in a terrace on the north side. Wouldn't that be satisfactory?

EMMA (*impulsively*). Oh, I'd want you to be more than that!

JOYCE (*ironically*). A member of Parliament. A leader-writer on the Freemen's Journal. A lecturer in the University. (EMMA *nods.*)

EMMA. But don't think I'm waiting for any offers from Stephen Daedalus.

JOYCE. When one loves one gives and that is all.

EMMA. And so for the sake of escaping what you call servility, you would not marry a girl who gave herself to you?

JOYCE. For me, there is no marriage.

EMMA. Why do you do this to me? I have admired you. I have told myself that there is no young man like you in the whole of Dublin.

JOYCE. I will be in your garden tonight. The glow will be in your face.

EMMA. Speak to me as a young man would speak to a girl, James Joyce.

JOYCE. I am a young man. You are a young woman. The great wind of humanity blows on us both.

EMMA. No. No. No. No. I go back to what I should do.

JOYCE. And what is that, Emma?

EMMA. Hand out my leaflets.

JOYCE. That is not what you came for, Emma. You came to have me make my approach to you.

EMMA. And your approach has been wrong, wrong. I will never again have a dream like the dream I had. Goodby, James Joyce.

JOYCE. I will be at your window and you will know I am there.

EMMA. It won't change me a bit to know you are there. (*She goes to the exit and then turns back.*) She would have to be like you.

JOYCE. She would have to love me and trust me.

EMMA. With her whole life?

JOYCE. With her whole life. I could ask for nothing less.

EMMA. And what would she ask for?

JOYCE. Freedom.

EMMA. Even to go with another man?

JOYCE. Surely.

EMMA. When will you meet her?

JOYCE. When we are both exiles.

EMMA. And you with your arrogance will not know what she is doing for you.

JOYCE. She will know that I am giving her freedom.

EMMA. Isn't it what you call freedom?

JOYCE. Separation from servility.

EMMA. She would be brave. There are girls like that. She will come to you because—oh, because there is something before you, James Joyce, that is great.

JOYCE. Emma! Emma! You came to me! Do not leave me like this! If you do, you leave one who is in despair! Who is with me? No one! No one! No one!

EMMA. May God be with you! (*She turns and goes.*)

JOYCE (*bitterly*). She is forgetting herself! That is something that should have been said to me in the pious language of our forefathers. And now? Stephen Daedalus among the Celtic ruins! Stephen Daedalus abandoned! A wirrasthrue! Wirrasthrue! And have I no one to turn to in this wide, earthy, god-forsaken world?

VOICE (*at back*). You know whom you can return to!

JOYCE. Did I not expect them? The Emissaries!

FIRST VOICE. Expected!

SECOND VOICE. Emissaries!

THIRD VOICE. Friends!

JOYCE (*troubled*). You will not let me go!

FIRST VOICE. Whether you go out into the world as James Joyce or Stephen Daedalus, you are still one of us.

JOYCE. A mutinous one, as you know.

SECOND VOICE. In the motions you have made towards the life of the artist, where have you gone for the formulation of your artistic creed?

JOYCE. Not to one who has the voice of the rabble.

THIRD VOICE. You went to the great and orthodox teacher we kept before you.

JOYCE. Yclept Tunbelly.

FIRST VOICE. You seem to think that the ideas that possess you at the present moment, ideas that belong, perhaps, to the fashions of today, to the adventurousness of youth, to personal isolation, to unhappy experiences, will not change. You think that in ten, in twenty years, you will be denying Christianity, you who accept no philosophy but a Christian one.

JOYCE. By Saint Stephen! You will have me again declare my mutiny!

SECOND VOICE. We do not look to you because you are one of the flock. No, for quite the opposite reason.

JOYCE. Ah, yes! Ah, yes! Ah, yes!

THIRD VOICE. We are called worldly by the worldly, as you know.

JOYCE. What can you do with one who declares he cannot live without women—without a woman?

FIRST VOICE. You would stay in the world and have the life of the world.

SECOND VOICE. You are a young man with a doubtful future.

THIRD VOICE. But with an unusual character.

JOYCE. You would make my future less doubtful?

FIRST VOICE. That could be done by us.

SECOND VOICE. There are people in the world who look to us.

THIRD VOICE. And for whom our recommendations are unquestionable.

JOYCE. Where a young man of unusual character would serve you?

FIRST VOICE. We would have you stay on friendly terms with us.

SECOND VOICE. In any country in the world you would care to live in.

THIRD VOICE. Already you know the humiliations of the office-seeker, the squalor of beginnings.

JOYCE. I could reach the life of the artist.

FIRST VOICE. We could open the way to it for you.

SECOND VOICE. Then you could sow your seeds in a regular furrow instead of casting them in a wilderness.

THIRD VOICE. A furrow entrusted to you.

JOYCE. By whom?

FIRST VOICE. By us whose philosophy you look to.

SECOND VOICE. Who uphold the order you yourself belong to.

THIRD VOICE. Who have never been unfriendly to the artist. (*A silence*)

JOYCE. I will break the silence. I have philosophy enough to know that there must be mutability. Many of the things that separate me from you, my mind will be changed about. But there is one place where there will be never a change. I will not serve.

FIRST VOICE. Whose service do you reject?

JOYCE. The Church. The State.

SECOND VOICE. Where then do you go?

JOYCE (*his hands on a tall stone, supporting himself*). Into exile. Into silence. Into cunning. *Non serviam.* Hawk that was driven here by the voice of the crowd, now show yourself to me!

VOICES. Remember! Remember! Remember!

JOYCE (*making a declaration*). *Non serviam!* (*Enter two middle-aged men. One is the man-about-town become shabby in his garb, but still sporting cane and eye-glass. He is* JOHN STANISLAUS JOYCE. *The other is bearded, spectacled, outgoing, with a touch of the public man about him. He is* MR. MACANASPEY.)

JOHN STANISLAUS. The verdict was that my hopeful son would be found here.

MACANASPEY. What do you think of the candidate's chance, John Stanislaus?

JOHN STANISLAUS. What I think of any of them is not for verbatim reporting.

MACANASPEY. The old spirit of faction showed itself as strong as ever, John Stanislaus.

JOHN STANISLAUS. And why the hell wouldn't it? The only one who could keep them in order is gone from us. (*Puts handkerchief to his eyes*) Parnell! Parnell! Do you know who I saw in the crowd? If you can believe it, MacAnaspey, no other than the hag that threw lime into the chieftain's eyes.

MACANASPEY. But that was at the Kilkenny election, John Stanislaus.

JOHN STANISLAUS. There's nothing to prevent such hags going the length and breadth of Ireland.

MACANASPEY. Nothing! Nothing! Nothing!

JOHN STANISLAUS. You say it as solemnly as one of the old monks who were here, brother MacAnaspey.

MACANASPEY. To come in here where, I venture to say, there was never a voice raised in dispute.

JOHN STANISLAUS. Then the monks weren't Irish, that's all. And what about our jollification?

MACANASPEY (*rather anxiously*). With your son to share it, I hope.

JOHN STANISLAUS. Where is he? (*Seeing* JOYCE) Would you tell me why he's standing there, looking to the top of the tower?

MACANASPEY. Do you know, John Stanislaus, that a thought came to me when I was listening to the speeches.

JOHN STANISLAUS. God forgive you if it was a worse thought than I had. Well, I'm between a son watching the jackdaws and a fellow-mortal who has the price of a jollification, and what can I do but listen.

MACANASPEY (*brightly*). I believe that what we were listening to is all in the past.

JOHN STANISLAUS. Don't keep our jollification in the too distant future. I'm off to have a word with mine host. Follow me to the hotel — I hear it's a good one — with Jim. (*He goes.* JOYCE *comes towards* MR. MACANASPEY.)

JOYCE. Mr. MacAnaspey! (*with dignity*)

MACANASPEY (*with some deference*). The same, young sir. Your father has gone to prepare — in his sporting phrase — a jollification.

JOYCE. And who will provide?

MACANASPEY. Myself.

JOYCE. You entreat us kindly, Mr. MacAnaspey.

MACANASPEY. I was in your audience when you addressed the Historical Society on the poet, James Clarence Mangan. A noble, I might say, a prophetic discourse.

JOYCE. Thanks be to God!

MACANASPEY. What did you say, young sir?

JOYCE. Thanks be to God that I had one attentive listener.

MACANASPEY. Surprisingly — to me at least — you did not speak of that tremendous poem, "The Nameless One."

JOYCE (*distantly*). An oversight.

MACANASPEY. I should have liked to hear you respect in your

melodious voice—and indeed I was entranced by the melody of your voice—that verse so deep in feeling.

> Go, tell them how, with genius wasted,
> Betrayed in friendship, befooled in love,
> With spirit, shipwrecked, with young hopes blasted,
> He still, still strove.

(JOYCE *moves away.*) Many of us would have been stirred deeply by your rendering of that great verse that has the history of the man in it—

> And he fell far through that pit abysmal,
> The gulf and grave of Maginn and Burns,
> And pawned his soul for the devil's dismal
> Stock of returns.

But your address was so inspired and inspiring that it was not until you had seated yourself that I realized you had not mentioned "The Nameless One."

JOYCE. The hawk has come down. (*He looks to where the hawk has alighted on top of the cross.*) (MACANASPEY *takes off his glasses, wipes them and puts them back.*)

MACANASPEY (*looking towards the cross*). It is a hawk.

JOYCE (*speaking in rhythmic tone*). He will stay long enough for me to speak—to speak and so pledge myself to silence, to cunning, to exile. I am Stephen Daedalus. I go to forge in the smithy of my soul the uncreated conscience of my race!

MACANASPEY (*enthusiastically*). Your tone of voice is superb!

JOYCE. May I know how we've been brought together?

MACANASPEY. Your father and I—in the natural way of meeting here and there.

JOYCE. Here and there! City streets! People not finding themselves.

MACANASPEY. But this is fateful, young sir.

JOYCE. In what way and why?

MACANASPEY. You will hear . . .

JOYCE. At the jollification, no doubt.

MACANASPEY. Here is the place! Where the cross stands with its
circle.

JOYCE. Ah! Your epiphany, MacAnaspey.

MACANASPEY. I have to make a preface or preamble.

JOYCE. Make it.

MACANASPEY. Out there with your father. . . . The memory of
your discourse came to me. I knew there are men in Ireland who
would be heard from. The young man who delivered the address on
Mangan. Men like him. Poets. Historians. Philosophers.

JOYCE. Heard from!

MACANASPEY. Who would bring something into the mind of the
people that would make all that seem—what it is—senseless.

JOYCE (quoting in a voice that has a chant in it). "Why do you fly
from our torches which were made out of the wood of the tree under
which Christ wept in the Garden of Gethsemane? Why do you fly
from our torches which were made of the sweet wood after it had
vanished from the world, and come to us who made it of old times
with out breath?"

MACANASPEY. I don't understand it, young sir.

JOYCE. It is by our only poet, Yeats.

MACANASPEY. The public does not understand him.

JOYCE. I believe the public will change him.

MACANASPEY. And you, young sir?

JOYCE. Exile and memory! Memory and exile! From them there
will be creation.

MACANASPEY. I believe in your prophecy.

JOYCE. What prophecy?

MACANASPEY. The prophecy that was in your voice when you spoke of Mangan . . . Poets, historians, philosophers. They will come. They will succeed the factionists. It is they who will make "flames wrap hill and word." Yourself among them, young sir.

JOYCE. You believe in Ireland?

MACANASPEY. Yes, and when something that has spirit appears all that will go. The way you spoke of James Clarence Mangan made that plain to me. Even though the "Nameless One" had no place in what you said. Poets, historians, philosophers, the call has come for you to take over. Standing by this cross I tell you so.

JOYCE. In the smithy of my soul . . .

MACANASPEY. What do you say, young sir?

JOYCE. I have rejected. I have been rejected. I am hungry and thirsty.

MACANASPEY (*heartily*). This way, young sir.

JOYCE. To the jollification?

MACANASPEY. Your father waits for us.

JOYCE. And Mentor send me to him. (*They go off.*)

(*The* TWO HOODED FIGURES *appear. They stand by the entrance and speak rhythmically.*)

FIRST FIGURE. An exile, he who sang
       'I am of Ireland,
       And Ireland's holy land.'
       And though his name be lost,
       These words of his, brought back,
       Have sweetened bitter times.

SECOND FIGURE. The shapeless granite bulks
       Where furrow loses ground:
       A man his chisel takes,
       And makes of it a shape

To make men know that man,
Is not the transient men.

FIRST FIGURE. Oppressed such man may be,
And heedless in some choice,
But venerate him still,
He only can draw men
To live the sacred hours.
Only his work has worth.

CURTAIN

SELECTED PLAYS OF PADRAIC COLUM was composed in 10-point Digital Compugraphic
Baskerville and leaded 2 points by Metricomp; with display type set in Folkwang by J. M. Bund-
scho, Inc.; and ornaments supplied by Jöb Litho Services; printed by sheet-fed offset on 55-pound,
acid-free Glatfelter Antique Cream, and smyth sewn and bound over binder's boards in Joanna
Arrestox B by Maple-Vail Book Manufacturing Group, Inc.; with dust jackets printed in 2 colors
by Philips Offset Company, Inc.; designed by Mary Peterson Moore; and published by Syracuse
University Press, Syracuse, New York 13244-5160.